# Just ask

# Jon Eakes

READER'S DIGEST

# Just ask

# Jon Eakes

THE READER'S DIGEST ASSOCIATION (CANADA) LTD.
Montreal

**Project Editor**
Andrew Jones

**Editor**
Robert Ronald

**Art Director**
John McGuffie

**Designer**
Cécile Germain

**Production**
Holger Lorenzen

**Copy Editors**
Gilles Humbert
Joseph Marchetti

**Indexer**
Linda Cardella Cournoyer

**Vice President,
Books & Home Entertainment**
Deirdre Gilbert

Published in Canada in 1997 by The Reader's Digest Association (Canada) Ltd.
215 Redfern Avenue, Westmount, Quebec H3Z 2V9

For information on this and other Reader's Digest products or to request a catalogue, please call our 24-hour Customer Service hotline at 1-800-465-0780.

You can also visit us on the World Wide Web at
http://www.readersdigest.ca

**Canadian Cataloguing in Publication Data**

Eakes, Jon
      Just ask Jon Eakes

Accompanied by a CD-ROM
ISBN 0-88850-608-2

      1. Dwellings—Maintenance and repairs—Amateurs' manuals. I. Reader's Digest Association (Canada) II. Title

TH4817.3.E23 1997      643'.7      C97-900879-4

Printed in Canada

97 98 99 00 / 5 4 3 2 1

# Foreword

In my 20 years of home improvement work, hosting Life Network's *Just Ask Jon Eakes* has been the most fun for me. I love being able to talk directly with you, homeowners, getting to the root of your problems, sometimes common, sometimes unique. Being able to use computer graphics to answer your questions live is as close as I can get to a face-to-face meeting.

Following your requests, I have put many of the most important questions and answers that you have asked me into this book, placing the cream of three seasons of home repair knowledge at your fingertips, and your computer's mouse—I could not resist creating a whole series of computer animations to try and explain some of the more complex aspects of how our houses work and how we can maintain them. You can find them—and much more—on the free CD-ROM at the back of this book.

The show goes on, as they say, and this is a work in progress. People constantly ask me how do I know so much. My honest reply is that I am kept humble by the quantity of new information I learn every week, from you and the specialists I refer to when looking for answers. Something mystifies you about your house? Log on to the Reader's Digest website or tune into Life Network and keep asking me those tough questions. Together we can continue to improve the quality of housing across Canada.

—*Jon Eakes*

# Contents

## Chapter 1
## Basements & Foundations — 30

## Chapter 2
## Walls & Floors — 40

# Introduction

A modern house is more than the sum of its parts. As we insulate, seal, and ventilate our homes for greater comfort and energy efficiency, we are discovering that the various elements of our homes are becoming more and more interconnected. Replacing the windows can block off cold air drafts, which can lead to higher humidity in the house. Higher humidity can increase condensation in the bedroom windows,

a perfect breeding ground for mold, an invisible health hazard. To get rid of the mold, we require better ventilation in the house, as well as air cleaners to keep the air healthy. But how do we control the flow of heated air in the house, especially after we insulate the basement? The connections go on and on. We call this concept the "House as a System." Understanding your house in its entirety rather than as separate areas can help you create that comfortable, trouble-free home you have dreamed of.

*Just Ask Jon Eakes* is designed to make sense of this complex web of connections. While the book is thematically arranged into 10 chapters—from Basements and Foundations through Roofing and Siding—the answers to many of the questions have some degree of impact on another area in the house, encouraging you to look at not just the immediate problem in isolation, but as part of your home's big picture. For example, the reason your walls are discolored may have just as much to do with the insulation behind the wall as the quality of the air and the temperature inside the room. Or how installing a ceiling fixture can affect the degree of condensation in your attic.

The *Just Ask Jon Eakes* CD-ROM included with the book takes the House as a System concept to a whole new level. Walk around a 3-D house and explore the different areas by clicking on the pop-up menus in the home screen. Click on the videocassettes in each closeup screen for state-of-the-art computer animations that illustrate questions and their answers in striking detail.

Scrolling text with each animation examines the problem and possible solutions in greater technical depth, a series of related questions help place the question or problem in context to the rest of the house, and the resource pages help you get down to brass tacks with information on specific products and how to use them. You will even find hot links that connect your web browser directly to a wide variety of Internet websites for more information and resources on home renovation products, research, and publications, even the Life Network and Reader's Digest websites. So kick off your shoes, start up your computer, and see how *your* house works.

# General Repairs

## Aviation snips

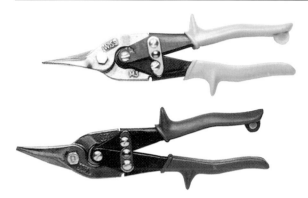

Cut sheet metal with less effort than tin snips. Their pointed noses make cutting odd shapes easy, and their serrated jaws prevent slippage and withstand heavy use. All aviation snips cut straight lines; specific heads can also cut left curves, right curves, and a combination of all three cuts.

## Screwdrivers

Robertson screwdriver, usually color-coded according to size, can reach screws that are sunk below the surface in furniture. The square drive provides high torque power. Recommended sizes: #6, #8, #10.

Phillips screwdriver, the most common type of cross-head screwdriver, fits snugly into a Phillips-head screw. The cross design of the tip provides a better grip than a slotted screwdriver. Recommended sizes: small, medium, and large.

Standard (slotted) screwdriver fits slotted screws. The flared tip *(left)* works best on round- or oval-headed screws. Recommended sizes: small, medium, and large.

## Electrician screwdriver

Made with a long shank to reach deep in electrical boxes, this screwdriver is perfect for electrical work. Plastic tube around the shank protects the user from electric shock. Always unplug appliance or disconnect power before doing any electrical work.

## Chalk line

A case, filled with chalk and 15 m to 30 m (50–100 ft) of line on a reel, marks a long, straight line between two points. Pull the line from the case, hold it taut, and snap it to leave a chalk mark as a guide. Can also be used as a plumb bob. The longest straightedge you can buy.

## Electronic stud finder

Locates studs behind wall coverings by measuring changes in the wall's density. Can be expensive; inexpensive magnetic finders that react to the screws or nails that secure wall coverings to the studs are also available. Either type can be thrown off by wires or pipes in walls.

## Torpedo level

Short, 20 cm (8 in.) version of the longer carpenter's level. Good for plumbing repairs because it fits into most restricted spaces. Tape it to a long, straight board for a fairly accurate larger level. Some models are grooved for resting on pipes and shafts.

## Retractable tape

Stores a spring-loaded metal rule in a small case. A hook on the end of the rule usually catches on a workpiece, making long measurements a one-person job. Most models feature a locking mechanism to prevent retraction and a belt clip. Recommended length: 4.8 m (16 ft).

## Profile gauge

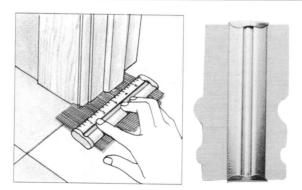

Duplicates and transfers an irregular design to a template or piece of stock. Uses a series of moving metal or plastic pins that take on the contour of whatever object they are pressed against. A great gadget for detail work.

## Standard electric hand drill

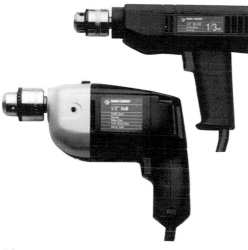

Comes with 6, 9.5, and 12 mm ($^1/_4$, $^3/_8$, and $^1/_2$ in.) chucks to hold bits. Select a reversible model so you can back out bits or loosen screws. While a 12 mm ($^1/_2$ in.) drill can bore larger holes, a 9.5 mm ($^3/_8$ in.) variable speed reversible drill *(upper left)* can handle most home repairs.

## Bits

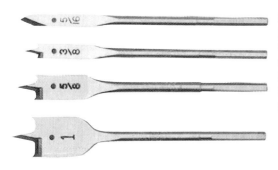

Spade bits feature center locating point and two sharp flat cutting edges which work, with a scraping action, to bore holes in wood. Useful for drilling large holes, although they tend to leave splintered exit holes.

Twist bits are made for wood and metal. For wood, use twist bits made of carbon steel; for metal, choose bits made of high-speed steel, and lubricate the drilling surface with machine oil.

## Files

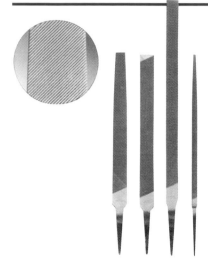

Flat file *(far left)*, a general-purpose file for fast removal of metal. Has a slightly tapered shape and double-cut faces, with a single cut along the edges. Good for keeping paint scrapers clean and sharp.

Hand file *(far center)*. Similar to flat file, but with parallel edges; one edge is *safe*, or uncut, to prevent marring the work.

Pillar file *(near center)*. A thin file, fits into narrow grooves and slots.

Square file *(near right)*. Shaped to fit into recesses, angles, and holes for filing. Like the flat file, it tapers toward the end.

## Sandpaper discs

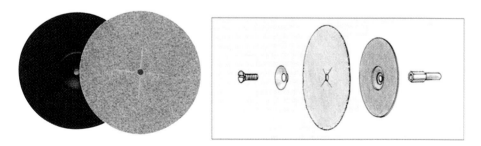

Convert an electric hand drill into a sander. Some discs are used in combination with a backer pad and arbor. Some systems work with self-adhesive sandpaper discs or have a hook-and-loop backing. Sandpaper discs are available with garnet and aluminum oxide, and with coarse through fine grits. Good for general cleaning and surface removal.

## General-purpose saw

Makes both crosscuts and rip cuts in wood. Its teeth have three beveled sides, which provide razor-sharp cutting. Deep gullets between the teeth make it easier to clear chips away fast. Blade is typically 65 cm (26 in.) long with 9 teeth per inch. Ideal if you only have one saw.

## Scrolling saber saw

Saber saw with a pivoting blade holder for cutting intricate curves and contours without the operator turning the body of the saw. A wide range of blades is available; the narrower the blade, the tighter the turning radius. Next to the electric hand drill, this is the second most basic power tool in a homeowner's toolbox. With the right blade, it will cut through anything.

## Glass cutter

Scores lines in glass. Separate the glass by holding it on each side of the score with your thumbs and index fingers and bending it until it snaps. Notches can be used to cut thin strips.

## Edge clamps

Has two or three screws extending from the frame to exert right-angle pressure on the edge or side of a workpiece. The right-angle, or center, screw can be positioned on or off center on varying thicknesses of workpieces. Good for gluing trim or edge banding on countertops.

## Straight-jaw locking pliers

Clamp firmly onto objects. A knob in one handle controls the jaws' width and tension. Close handles to lock the pliers; release a lever to open them. Indispensable around the house.

## Hand stapler

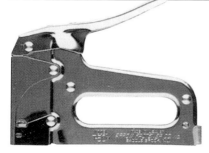

Drives staples with a squeeze of the handle. Use it to attach paper-covered insulation, hang plastic sheets, install screening, or for any major stapling job in your home. Specialty models are available for wiring and upholstery.

# Round-nose pliers

Favored by electricians, these pliers have smooth, tapered, round jaws designed for bending thin wire and sheet metal into different-sized loops. Excellent for wiring electrical boxes, outlets, and appliances.

# Multipurpose electrician's pliers

Measure, cut, and strip wire; also crimp wire connectors and cut machine screws. As with other wire strippers, handles do not insulate against electricity. A must for all wiring jobs.

# Major Project Essentials

## Circular saw

Used for fast straight cuts in wood or other materials. Upper blade guard is fixed; lower guard is spring-loaded and retracts as the saw cuts into the work. Baseplate rests on the stock and can be angled up to 45°. Use combination blades for rip, miter and crosscuts, use plywood/ paneling blades for sheet goods. Recommended size: 18 cm ($7^1/_4$ in.).

## Sliding compound miter saw

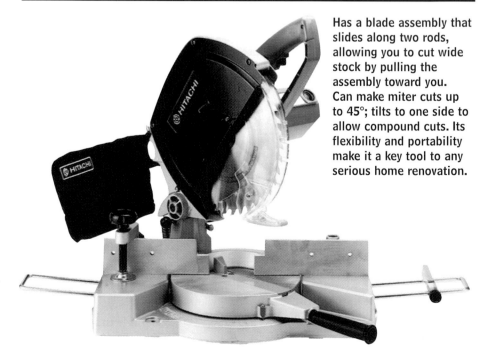

Has a blade assembly that slides along two rods, allowing you to cut wide stock by pulling the assembly toward you. Can make miter cuts up to 45°; tilts to one side to allow compound cuts. Its flexibility and portability make it a key tool to any serious home renovation.

## Portable work center

Combines a workbench, tool stand, vise, and sawhorse in one compact unit. Wide adjustable jaws clamp workpieces horizontally and vertically. V-grooves in the jaws help clamp pipe and tubing. When closed fully, the jaws form a workbench that locks at two heights for a multitude of tasks. Folds for convenient storage or transportation.

## Dead-blow hammer

Head is filled with steel shot and oil that absorb energy when the hammer impacts, eliminating any rebound in demolition and assembly work. Head weighs 240 g to 1.8 kg (8 oz–4 lb). If you are knocking things apart, this will double your power.

## Quick-Grip™ bar clamp

Has a movable jaw with a pistol-shaped handle. To slide the jaw, pull the trigger near the handle; squeeze the grip to apply jaw pressure. The jaws have removable rubber pads to protect surfaces. Additional corner pads help in clamping right-angle joints.

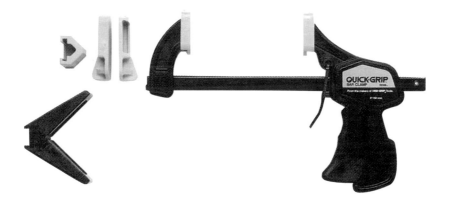

## Skate-wheel jointer

Rakes out mortar to a depth of 12 mm ($^1/_2$ in.) from a joint. The length of the nail that scrapes out the mortar can be adjusted to change the appearance of the joint. Good for taking the right amount of mortar out from between two bricks for repointing. After raking, smooth and compress the joint with a narrow jointer.

# Standard router

Used for top-quality joinery and making decorative edges or surfaces. For light tasks, choose a standard $^{7}/_{8}$ hp model with a 6 mm ($^{1}/_{4}$ in.) collet. Invest more in router bits than in the router itself to start; buy carbide-tipped bits as they require less sharpening and last longer than high-speed steel bits. Recommended bits: rabbeting, beading, dovetail, chamfer, roundover, ogee, three-wing slotting cutter.

# Hole saw

Tempered hardened-steel teeth cut large holes in wood, metal, and sheet goods. Saw is mounted on a hole-saw arbor *(far right)*; the arbor is inserted into a drill. Great for door handles and locks.

# Plumbing

## Pipe wrench

Turns threaded pipes. The upper jaw is adjusted by turning the knurled knob. Both jaws have serrated teeth for gripping power. When using the wrench, turn it so that  you apply pressure on the movable jaw. That jaw is spring-loaded and slightly angled; it allows you to release the grip and reposition the wrench, without readjusting the jaw, when you remove the pressure.

## Pipe or tubing cutter

Produces clean cuts on copper or steel pipe or tubing. Cutters come in sizes to fit pipes and tubing of different diameters. Some cutters, such as the one at center, feature a built-in reamer to remove burrs after cutting.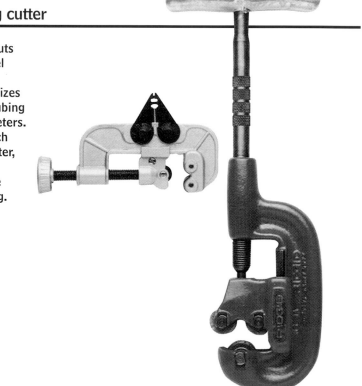

## Propane torch

Uses propane gas that mixes with the surrounding air to produce a hot flame (temperature about 1371°C/2500°F). Different tips are available for soldering, removing paint, and other jobs requiring localized heat. Always use lead-free, solid-core solder when working with water pipes.

## Basin wrench

A plumbing tool for removing and installing sink faucets. Has a long handle that reaches up from under a sink to turn nuts on fittings and faucets. The hinged jaw repositions itself after each turn. Buy one with a reversible jaw. The secret to easy sink installations.

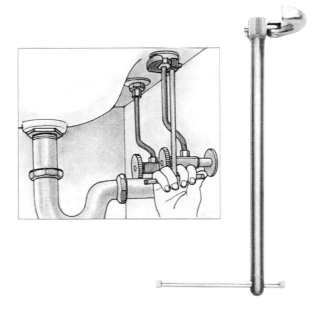

# Painting

## Painter's five-in-one tool

Blade functions as a paint scraper, putty remover and spreader, gouger, and paint-roller cleaner. Useful for making repairs, installing window glass, painting, and hanging wall coverings. The best choice for scraping paint off paint rollers.

## Brush and roller-cover spinner

Cleans paint brushes or rollers. Mount a brush or roller cover on the spindle and soak in water or appropriate cleaning solvent. Inside a large garbage can or in an area protected by drop cloths, pump the handle to spin the brush or cover dry. Cuts your cleaning time in half.

## Trim guard

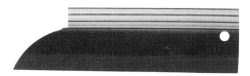

Keeps paint off adjoining straight surfaces. Hold it perpendicular to the work with the long edge touching it; the roller cover should fit into its curved shape to let you apply paint to the edge of the work.

## Paint glove

For applying paint to unusually-shaped items, such as spindles. Dip the glove into the paint, then spread the paint onto the work.

## Heat gun

Focuses a controlled amount of heat, usually between 121°C (250°F) and 593°C (1100°F), to soften paint so you can remove it with a scraper. (Do not use on old, lead-based paint.) Start with a low temperature and work your way up.

## Pipe roller

Features an indented center groove in the cover to conform to the contour of heating pipes. Make sure you apply only heat-resis-tant paint to the pipe.

# Safety

We all know many of the basic safety precautions involved in home improvement work, even though we don't always follow them to the letter: placing ladders safely, ventilating rooms when using strong solvents, wearing gloves with caustic products, even occasionally putting on those safety glasses. Hard hats and steel-toed work boots are not seen much around home-improvement sites, although they probably should be. We have long believed that accidents only happen to others.

But the world is changing. If you followed the evolution of professionals on construction sites, you would be surprised to realize to what extent far-reaching safety measures are being used today by men and women who, only 15 years ago, considered ear protectors a nuisance to use. We have learned a great deal about the long-term effects of the tools, techniques, and products we work with, and much of this knowledge is now commonly available to homeowners for their routine projects.

To begin with, many traditionally hazardous products such as solvents, paints, and glues now have much safer, water-based counterparts that cut down on noxious fumes. When you must deal with dust or solvent fumes, you can now find a range of good masks, from cotton to carbon-filtered, at all large hardware stores. You should use earplugs with all loud equipment.

Your shoes should have a good grip and protect you from falling objects, and you should always wear a hard hat when working under things that might fall. Back-support belts for lifting are now commonly available as well.

The best tips I can give you on working safety are simply to slow down and think ahead. Work with sharp tools and firm working surfaces. Check your local building and electrical codes. Most importantly, if you are not enjoying it, or if it appears you have a problem where you are in over your head, consider asking a pro to take over (see "Hiring A Professional" on page 175). Fatigue is probably the greatest safety hazard of all. So stop and smell the flowers—then go back to fixing the sewer pipe.

# BASEMENTS & FOUNDATIONS

# CHAPTER 1

Originally a humble root cellar, the basement has served a number of household roles over the years—storage area, laundry room, Dad's workshop. Yet more and more today we are asking this unfinished, underground space to be a comfortable living area, a trouble-free basement with a footing below the frost line, moisture proofing on the outside, full-height insulation on either the inside or the outside, and a drainage layer on the outside that directs water into a drain before it gets a chance to look for a crack in the wall.

The foundation—which carries the weight of the house, everything in it and everything sitting on the roof, right down to the soil—is being asked to do similar miracles. A good foundation does not sink, does not lift up with frost, does not crack, does not leak, and paint sticks to it without problems.

Since only new housing can deliver the perfect basement and foundation, most of us have to make do with what's downstairs. That said, you can accomplish a surprising amount just through simple moisture control. This chapter offers some answers to common questions about basements and foundations.

**Q** I am refinishing my basement. I have installed white polystyrene panels, but I am not sure whether or not I should install 2x4s directly over the polystyrene panels or if I should cut out strips of the panels to allow the 2x4s to be flush with the concrete wall behind the insulation. Which method is better?

**A** The first thing that you should be aware of is that white polystyrene insulation acts very much like fiberglass. It will absorb water, requires a vapor barrier, and needs to be protected. The blue or pink variety of this insulation is called rigid foam insulation, and does not absorb moisture. Therefore it does not require a vapor barrier. Both methods that you describe have their drawbacks. If you place the polystyrene blocks flush with the concrete wall and install the 2x4s over them, then you have lost some floor space. If you install the 2x4s first, and then place the polystyrene blocks in between the 2x4s, then you will have the tedious and time-consuming task of measuring, cutting, and installing numerous strips of insulation. There are other alternatives that are much easier to work with. The first is to install the 2x4s and place fiberglass over them, or use rigid foam insulation and a metal channel or wooden strapping staggered every 60 cm (2 ft). Using either of these eliminates the need for a stud wall. All that is required after that is the installation of drywall.

**Q** I live in a basement apartment with some rather noisy upstairs neighbors. Is there anything that I can do to better soundproof my apartment?

**A** There are two things that you can do to improve soundproofing. The easiest and least expensive method for soundproofing is to shoot some cellulose insulation between your drywall ceiling and your neighbor's floor joists. Cellulose insulation will cut down on the chatter of conversation as well as noise from the stereo and TV. If your neighbors have hardwood floors and a dog who scrapes his nails into the wood when he runs across the floor, then you will want something to protect against impact sounds. The best solution for someone living in a basement apartment is to install resilient bars. These are thin, Z-shaped bars of metal that attach to your ceiling on joists and against which you can attach a new drywall ceiling. The Z-bars are flexible and do not transmit impact noises. The insulation muffles the high frequencies, and the Z-bars the low frequencies. One last possibility that will definitely help is to ask your neighbors to lay a rug on their floor.

**Q** **Just how much insulation is really required in a basement?**

**A** How high an R-factor of insulation you put in your basement depends on where you live; simply check with local codes for the minimum ratings. However, if you want to create a comfortable living space that has heat and moisture control, you must insulate the whole wall right to the floor. Why? Concrete does little to stop heat flow and the soil doesn't help much until you get deep into the ground. Following the minimum ratings set by many local building codes and insulating only 60 cm (2 ft) below grade will make the basement a good storage space, but not comfortable enough to use as a living area; a bit like walking around in your Bermuda shorts in the snow. The best insulation job is done during new construction, with insulation on the outside from the foundation footings right up to the roof rafters covering the whole wall. During renovation, you can get similar results for the basement by insulating 60 cm (2 ft) into the soil and skirting 60 cm (2 ft) out, but this requires a lot of digging. If you are insulating from the inside, make sure to insulate the entire wall, and to cover the insulation in the joist area with a vapor barrier.

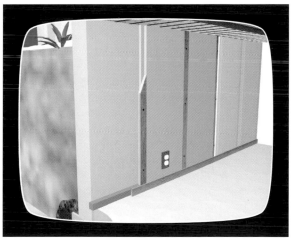

**For more detail, click on "Basement" on the home screen of the CD-ROM.**

33

**Q** We recently bought a house whose previous owners built a second-story addition. Unfortunately, they did not install a support wall. The result is that the ceiling above has sagged considerably in the middle. Is it possible to add support without having to install a support wall?

**A** Obviously, it is necessary to get some support for that addition. A complete support wall would be ideal, but if you want to avoid having to make two small rooms with the addition of the support wall, there is a solution. If you look in your basement there should be two or more columns that run in line with the support wall above. These columns, together with the beams they support, are doing the same job as a support wall. If you extended those columns from the floor to the ceiling below the addition and install a beam across the ceiling in line with the columns then you will have the support you need. The room will not be completely open, but with some interior design, it can maintain its open feeling.

**Q** I plan to install a bathroom and wood flooring in my unfinished basement. The concrete floor that is there now is very uneven. What should I do to even the concrete floor before installing the hardwood floor?

**A** Shimming up a wooden subfloor can take out some valuable headroom. There are two things to consider here: the degree of unevenness of the concrete floor and the height of the basement itself. If the degree of unevenness is 2.5 cm (1 in.) or less, the best solution is to use self-leveling concrete. It is much thinner than regular concrete and its slippery texture can be easily trowled out to a featheredge, where regular concrete has to be spread thick across the entire floor. Self-leveling concrete can be applied thickly where necessary, but more importantly, a very thin layer will hold. This way the entire floor can be coated with new concrete without losing too much headroom. Once the self-leveling concrete is cured, plywood can be glued and/or screwed into the concrete with or without foam insulation. Over that you can install hardwood floors, vinyl, or carpeting.

**Q** I am having a problem with the coating over my concrete foundation where the outside wall meets the grass. It has been flaking off. Is there a product that I can use to repair this?

**A** The coating that you are referring to is called parging. The reason that it is flaking off is because there has been a buildup of moisture and frost in that area. Rain gutters and proper landscaping will help in the future. In the meantime, to repair the parging take a hammer and bang away at the wall until all the loose material falls free. If it sounds hollow behind the wall, keep hammering until all the loose material falls. If it sounds solid, then the parging is attached and you can leave it alone. Once the wall has been freed of loose debris, apply a super-adhering primer specifically designed for parging. This will help guarantee that the new parging will stick to the old. The primer can be applied directly to the wall and the parging is then applied over the primer. If the parging is not already polymer-modified, the primer can also be used in place of the water to mix the parging as well. As with all wall construction and repair, a metal mesh will better hold the parging in place.

**Q** The stone wall in the basement of my 90-year-old house is constructed with an exposed wall of either cement or plaster that is crumbling and becoming very porous. What can I do to fix it?

**A** Your parging is crumbling because of excess water coming in from the outside. This is a problem that is common in houses built with stone walls. If your property's landscaping slopes toward the house, then rain, snow, and melting snow will flow toward—and into—the house. Similarly, if your rain gutters are dropping water directly beside the house and the water has nowhere to flow but back toward the house, it too will enter the house through your foundation. A third possible problem (but not as common as the first two) is that the water table directly underneath your house may be relatively high. Again, excess water from rain and melted snow in spring will force the water table higher, and unfortunately, into your house. Once you have corrected those problems, you can tackle the basement wall *(see question above)*.

**Q** My cottage is built on solid rock. Over the years I have encountered problems with moisture in the basement. In the past I have had to replace floor joists under the first floor. I am sure that the moisture is coming from condensation and not seepage. Should I install a vapor barrier directly under the floor joists?

**A** If the cottage is built on solid rock then the problem is definitely not one of seepage. You do not want to put a vapor barrier just underneath the floor joists; this would only collect moisture in the winter and further damage the joists. You do want to install a vapor barrier, but on the unfinished basement floor. You should cover as much of the floor as possible, but it does not have to be completely covered. The amount of moisture entering the crawl space by evaporation is proportional to the surface area covered by the plastic. If 80 percent of the floor surface is covered by a vapor barrier, condensation will be reduced by 80 percent. Weigh down the vapor barrier with sand or some heavy rocks.

**Q** I want to insulate the crawl space in my basement. I was told that I should install a vapor barrier. Is this true?

**A** It is more important to place a moisture barrier on the dirt floor than to place a vapor barrier over the insulation. Plastic sheeting should be placed across the dirt floor of the crawl space and fiberglass insulation between the floor joists above. Under normal circumstances, a vapor barrier should be placed on the warm side of the insulation, but it is a very difficult job to undertake in such a small space. In your case, the floor above can act as the vapor retarder. Make sure that any small holes in the floor above are sealed completely, and if you have linoleum or vinyl flooring on the plywood, this will provide further vapor protection.

**Q** I plan to shut down my cottage for the winter, but I realize that some heat must be generated in the cottage to protect its foundation from frost damage. What is the ideal temperature for this?

**A** The simple answer to this question is that the temperature of the foundation must remain slightly above freezing. It does not have to be very much above, but it must be above. Frost problems often occur when clay soil is saturated with water and it freezes. It creates ice lenses that expand in the direction of heat loss. If the basement is not heated at all, these ice lenses expand toward the basement and can push the wall in. If the basement is heated to about 10°C (50°F), heat moves out from the basement and pushes the ice lenses harmlessly toward the surface of the soil.

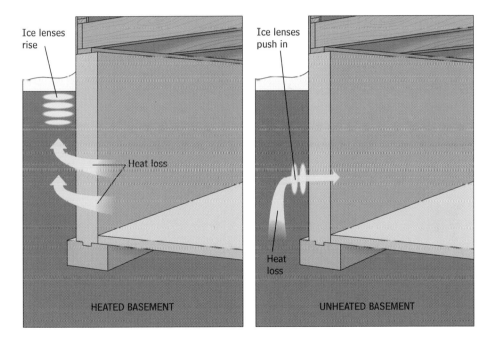

Ice lenses rise

Heat loss

HEATED BASEMENT

Ice lenses push in

Heat loss

UNHEATED BASEMENT

**Q** I am worried about potential frost problems in my basement. I recently completed some landscaping changes, and in the process exposed the footing of a concrete block wall about 4.5 m (15 ft) in length. The foundation was originally 1.2 m (4 ft) below grade, and it is now about 90 cm (3 ft) in depth. I have often heard that 1.2 m (4 ft) is the absolute minimum to prevent frost. Am I going to encounter problems, and if so, what can I do to prevent them?

**A** The reason that foundations are usually 1.2 m (4 ft) below grade is because 1.2 m (4 ft) of earth on the outside of a foundation is just enough to insulate the foundation against frost in most parts of Canada. There is a method that you can use that will allow you to have a shallow foundation without encountering any frost problems. Dig 60 cm (2 ft) down all around the problem area. Cover the wall with 5 cm (2 in.) of rigid

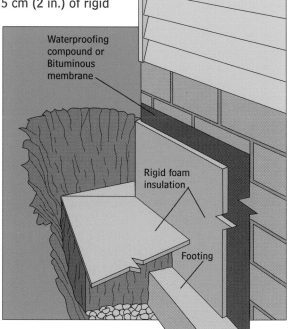

Waterproofing compound or Bituminous membrane

Rigid foam insulation

Footing

foam insulation and then skirt out 60 cm (2 ft) from the wall. A little soil and rigid foam insulation together will insulate the footings as if they were 1.2 m (4 ft) in the ground, and will keep them frost-free.

**Q** The brick foun-dation in the basement of my house built in 1920 has been flaking over the last year. Along with the flaking, there is a fine white powder that is falling to the ground. I plan to scrape the loose material from the foundation with a wire brush and then apply some bleach to remove any mold. What kind of paint should be applied that will allow moisture to evaporate?

**A** First of all, be very careful when using the wire brush that you remove only the loose material. Even though foundation brick is stronger than outside brick walls, it is still a relatively soft material. Secondly, make sure that you use muriatic acid as your cleaning material. There are several reasons for using this. It will etch into the brick a little bit and better prepare it for the coat of paint. It will also neutralize any alkyds in the mortar and brick that can prevent the paint from bonding to the surface. Since you want the paint to be able to breathe, you have two choices. The easier, but not as durable, method is to apply an exterior latex paint. A longer-lasting choice is a cementitious paint. This thick and creamy mixture has portland cement mixed in, and will bond to the surface much better than regular paint.

**Q** I bought a very old house that has a cement floor in an unfinished base-ment. There are some cracks and some crum-bling on both the walls and floor. Before I paint the walls and floor, I need to know how to prepare the surface, and once that is done, what kind of paint should I apply?

**A** If there is serious crumbling on the surface then no paint will stick very well. If the crumbling is minor, then start by gently scrubbing the surface with a wire brush. If you apply too much pressure, a lot will fall out. Just eliminate what is truly loose. The next step depends on what kind of paint you plan to apply. To prepare the sur-face for acrylic paint, first etch the walls and floor with muriatic acid. The acid will also clean off the surface some of the fine dust that was not removed with the wire brush. If you plan to apply latex, do the same thing, but use phosphoric acid instead of muriatic acid. Remember, if you choose either an acrylic or a latex paint, you will have to first apply a primer. Another possibility is to use a cementitious paint *(above)*. There are several different brands on the market. If you choose, you can even add color to cementitious paint.

# WALLS & FLOORS

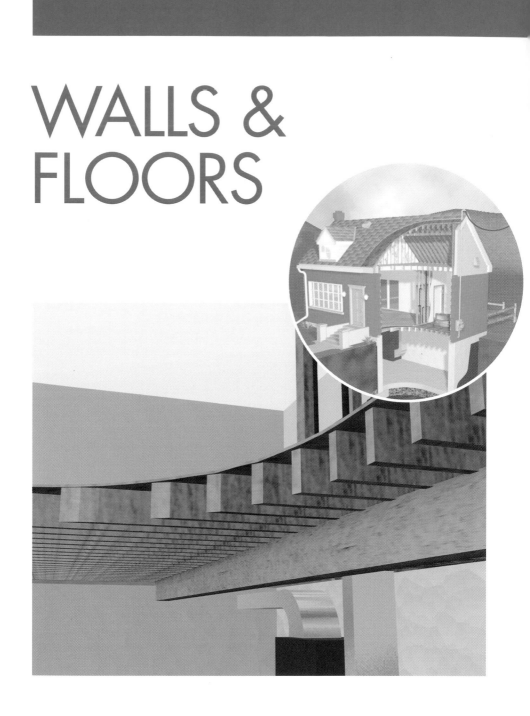

# CHAPTER 2

Walls, floors, and ceilings are probably the parts of the house that we see the most and that we notice the least—until they give us problems.

Walls and ceilings are not just surfaces for designer paints, wallpaper, and hanging decorations. They are also the inner layer of a rather amazing assembly of elements that allow us to survive the harsh Canadian winter and be comfortable in the summer. However, if the house moves, they crack. If the insulation fails, they get cold. If moisture accumulates, they can get downright moldy. Walls and ceilings require maintenance and an understanding of the forces attacking them. Be kind to them as they are your last line of defense against the weather. When they show signs of stress, look behind them for the causes.

Floor coverings are supposed to stand up to everything we can drop on or drag over them. The floor structure itself is supposed to be flat, rigid, and not squeak despite all the strange things we have done in the joist area below (not to mention the radical changes in humidity that some houses experience from August through January). As the questions that follow demonstrate, with the right upkeep, your floors can do just that.

**Q** I have a 30-year-old house with stucco exterior walls. I want to cover the walls with vinyl siding, but I have no idea what is between the stucco exterior walls and the interior drywalls. Is it necessary to insulate before installing the vinyl siding?

**A** This is a great opportunity to insulate your house effectively. Insulating walls can be a laborious and expensive project, but if you need to change the siding anyway, insulation is an easy add-on. If you do not know what is in between the walls, simply drill a hole and find out. In the end the hole will not matter because you will be covering it with the siding. If the house is about 30 years old, when you punch a hole through the wall you will likely find the space between the walls filled with fiberglass. If it is not, then this is the first thing that you should do. After you have sealed the hole, apply 2.5 cm (1 in.) thick sheets of rigid foam insulation over the stucco exterior walls. Over that install the vinyl siding. You will then have a double layer of insulation that can definitely end up reducing your heating costs.

**Q** I recently bought a 10-year-old house. A stucco wall runs from the basement ceiling halfway down the wall. I want to extend the wall to the floor, but the existing wall has insulation behind it. How can I remedy the situation?

**A** Install a stud wall from the end of the existing wall to the floor and make sure that you put insulation behind the wall. Apply a vapor barrier over the stud wall and then install a drywall over that. At this point you have two choices: You can remove the existing stucco and then apply new stucco to the entire wall, or you can keep the existing stucco and add new stucco to the new section of the wall. If you choose the latter, the stucco may not have a uniform texture and the color of the new stucco may be slightly different from the old. A simple solution to this problem is to install some horizontal wood trim over the line where the old and new walls meet.

**Q** There are what appear to be water marks running down from the corners where the wall and ceiling meet in my one-story bungalow. There are mildew spots in the same areas. What can I do?

**A** I am almost certain that the two corners you are referring to are the northeast and northwest corners, where the house receives the least amount of sunlight. Without the sun, the drywall in those corners is colder and that reacts with the house's normal humidity, causing the mildew and excess moisture. The first thing that you should do is clean the wall using bleach to kill the mold. Then you should determine if there is too much humidity in the house or if the affected area is just too cold. The easiest way to check this is to look at your windows. If they are foggy most of the time, then there is likely too much humidity and you will have to better ventilate the house. If the windows are clear, then the problem lies with the temperature in the affected corners, and you will have to add insulation over the affected area to warm it up. One easy way to do this is to open up the soffits and put rigid foam insulation on the outside of the house over the affected area.

**Q** My master bedroom is one of the coldest rooms in the house. The back wall of the closet in the bedroom faces an outer wall, and there is a layer of frost that lines the top of that wall. The problem does not exist in any other room in the house. What is causing it and what can I do to get rid of the frost?

**A** The natural circulation of air in a room hits and warms the walls in the room. The back wall of the closet, however, is not exposed to that heat because it is being blocked by a door. The result is that the closet is colder than the rest of the room. There is probably a lack of insulation at the top of the wall as well, making it cold enough to create frost. There are several things that can be done. Caulk the wall to the floor behind the floor boards, or install some rigid foam insulation on the far wall in the closet and put up some drywall over that. Both measures will reduce the heat being lost outside and thus the amount of cold air entering the closet. In order to increase air circulation, which is a big part of the problem, cut off the bottom 5 cm (2 in.) or so of the closet door and install a vent above the door. These steps should prevent the frost from returning.

**Q** I could never quite figure out where a vapor barrier should go, and now my renovator is talking to me about an air barrier. What's the difference between the two?

**A** Air barriers and vapor barriers are elements of the house shell designed to help us to control moisture from causing damage in our houses. Sometimes they can be the same thing, like a sealed polyethylene sheet, sometimes they are installed separately. A vapor barrier (often called a vapor retarder because it doesn't keep *all* the moisture out) is a sheet of material (usually polyethylene plastic) installed on the "warm in winter" side of the insulation that prevents household moisture from filtering right through wallboard and on to the cold side of the insulation, where it could condense and cause mold and rot. However, since large quantities of water can infiltrate walls through air drafts, protecting your house from moisture also demands that you not let air wander in and out of your walls and attics. This is where air barriers come in. They can be a whole system of sealing your house on the inside, such as making electrical boxes, window frames, and floor joints airtight. Air barriers can also be sheathing or housewrap paper on the outside of the house. If the air barrier is on the cold side of the envelope, it must not be a vapor barrier at the same time; that is, it must stop air but let water vapor filter through it to allow a wet wall to dry out. All of this is complicated, but necessary, in our cold climate.

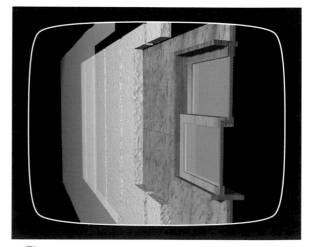

For more detail, click on "Walls" on the home screen of the CD-ROM.

**Q** I want to cover the main beam in the basement, which is a steel I-beam, with drywall. I don't know how to attach the drywall to the I-beam without drilling holes into the steel beam. Is this possible?

**A** The ingenious way around this problem is to use metal drywall corner beads. Screw corner beads to the floor joists overhead alongside the I-beam. Cut drywall strips 2.4 m (8 ft) long that are wide enough to cover the side of the beam. Screw and glue these to the corner beads above. Screw another corner bead to the bottom of all the drywall strips, then screw a piece of drywall across the bottom of the beam to the corner beads. Double the corners with another corner bead over the exposed corners, screwing through the drywall to the first corner bead, and your I-beam is out of sight, out of mind.

**Q** One of the vertical 2x4s in a stud wall in my hallway has bellowed to one side. How do I straighten out the 2x4, and can it be done by tearing down only one side of the stud wall?

**A** Yes it can be done exposing only one side of the wall. The standard method for correcting this problem is to saw into the 2x4 on the inside bellow. Do not saw all the way through. You do not want to cut the 2x4 into two pieces. After sawing about two-thirds of the way through, hammer in a wood wedge. This will actually lengthen the one side of the stud and straighten it out. Once it is straight, screw straps to both sides of the stud to restore its rigidity and strength.

**Q** How do I prevent the wallboard behind the bathroom tiles from swelling up?

**A** When water repeatedly gets into ordinary gypsum board, it softens and disintegrates, causing ceramic tiles to bulge or fall off. The key defense is to prevent the water from getting in. That means use a good grout and maintain it with regrouting when it cracks and silicone sealer every couple of years. The caulking between the tub and the tile must be continuous and remain flexible or water will get in there also. Use flexible caulk as well in the corner where the two walls come together to allow for building or panel movement. Install the wallboard 6 mm ($^1/_4$ in.) above the tub so that minor leaks won't have a chance to soak into the gyps. Using water-resistant panels gives you a greater margin for error and using special cement-board panels will avoid all future problems.

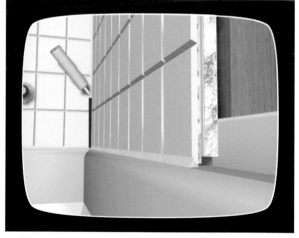

 For more detail, click on "Interiors" on the home screen of the CD-ROM.

**Q** One wall in the bedroom of my 20-year-old house has what appears to be masking tape peeling from the drywall. The tape has popped through the paint covering the wall. Is this masking tape, and what should I do to remove it?

**A** No, it is not masking tape but drywall tape. As you may know, drywall comes in sheets that measure 1.4 m x 2.4 m (4 ft x 8 ft). Where the sheets meet, the crack is covered with a plaster called drywall compound and reinforced with a special paper strip. This tape has no adhesive at all and relies on the compound to keep it glued to the wall. When there is not enough compound, or you have heavy condensation on the wall that could release the compound, the tape delaminates. Pry it open with a knife just enough to slide some white glue behind the tape. Hold it in place with masking tape for a day.

---

**Q** I am going to be installing some drywall in my basement. I know that tape has to be placed where two drywall panels meet. Should I use paper tape or fiberglass tape, and what is the difference between the two?

**A** There are differences between paper and fiberglass tape. The paper type is less expensive and works very well. It comes with a crease running down the middle that allows it to be folded at a 90° angle, which is ideal when working in corners. The fiberglass mesh does not fold as well, and is also very difficult to plaster smoothly over the top when it is not buried in a valley. It is, however, stronger, and works well when covering a wall crack with plaster, if you scrape out a valley to bury it. I use the old-fashioned paper tape for standard drywall applications.

**Q** What is the best way to fix major dents and holes in plaster or drywall?

**A** The answer depends on whether the patch has to withstand continued abuse or simply come out flat and smooth for painting. When you need to protect high-impact areas, like the lower part of a wall, I would use a hard filler like good old-fashioned Polyfilla™. Hard filler will sag under its own weight, so for large holes make it as thick as is workable and in small quantities. Moisten the area slightly for better adhesion. I prefer to avoid sanding a hard filler precisely because it is so hard and durable, so I always apply it flush or less, never over the top. If need be, apply several coats until it is almost flush although not quite smooth. Once it has set, which is pretty quick, apply a thin, pre-mixed finishing compound that is easy to feather and sand smooth. For patches where continued abuse is not a problem, a new breed of lighter plaster repair products on the market can make life even easier. Pre-mixed, lightweight, and very stiff, they will not sag or shrink. These compounds can be used outdoors or in the bathroom, where moisture poses a problem with most plasters. When applying, smooth them out with a spatula to avoid most of the sanding.

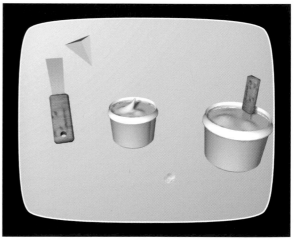

 **For more detail, click on "Interiors" on the home screen of the CD-ROM.**

**Q** Our house was built in 1915. It has a number of cracks in the walls that run through several layers of paint and wallpaper. What can we do to eliminate them?

**A** Whether you strip off the old wallpaper and paint or not, make a flat valley over the crack about 7.5 cm (3 in.) wide and 3 mm ($^1/_8$ in.) deep using a paint scraper. This will create the space necessary for strong plaster and fiberglass tape. Moisten the existing plaster and embed the tape in a layer of fresh plaster. Make sure that the tape is slightly recessed from the wall surface because it will be difficult to sand. Finish the job with a couple of coats of drywall joint compound for a smooth finish flush with the wall.

**Q** There are a number of cracks on the walls in my bedroom. I patched up the cracks last summer, but they have returned. Is there a trick to prevent the cracks returning?

**A** If you fixed the wall just last year and the cracks have returned, it is because your house is moving. Controlling the water around the foundation may stop the annual cracking. If you cannot stop the movement, then hide it. My suggestion is to install new drywall over the existing one. If your house continues to move, cracks will appear, but they certainly would not appear the following summer. Another option is to install some paneling over the drywall. Paneling sheets come in 1.2 m x 2.4 m (4 ft x 8 ft) sheets, and in some cases come with attractive patterns. The panels themselves will not crack, but each sheet will move back and forth. There are two little tricks that can make that movement invisible: The first is to paint the existing drywall the same color as the panel that you will install. If and when the sheets move, the part of the drywall exposed will not be that noticeable. The other, cleaner, option is to install some wood trim over the space where the sheets meet. If the sheets move slightly underneath, the wood trim will keep that space covered.

**Q** There is a crack where two walls meet at a 90° angle in my bedroom. A year ago I filled the crack with plaster and then painted over the wall. I feel that I may have not filled the crack properly because the crack has since returned. What is the best way to handle this?

**A** Wall cracks often return because houses are constantly shifting. If you simply fill the crack with plaster and cover it with a coat of paint,

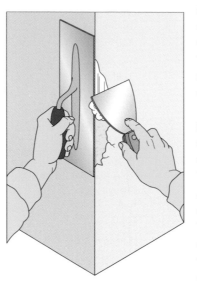

and the house expands and contracts with the changing seasons, the crack will likely return. You should first apply a fiberglass tape over the crack. This will provide a permanent seal over the crack. Then apply drywall filler and follow with a coat of paint.

**Q** I am living in a relatively new house. The wall in the vestibule has gathered a number of grooves and scratches caused by my dog's nails. How can I correct the problem and is it possible to avoid it in the future?

**A** The short-term solution is to plaster and paint the wall. Fill the grooves and scratches with plaster. After sanding, prime the surface with a primer sealer and paint over that. However, this solution will not prevent your dog from repeating his misdeeds. To prevent future abuse of the vestibule wall from pets, shoes, and boots, you can add what is called wainscoting. Found in many older homes, it is a panel of wood with molded trim that rises to the height of the chair rail above the floor (about 90 cm/3 ft) and protects the plaster underneath. As well as protection, wainscoting can add some decorative charm to any room.

**Q** I recently removed some old wood paneling that had been nailed to my basement walls. The wood paneling is removed, but there are a number of nails that are partially exposed but firmly embedded in the concrete block wall. What is the best way to get rid of the nails?

**A** There are three possible solutions to your problem. The first is the most difficult and that would involve cutting the nails where they enter the wall using an auto body grinder. This is difficult because the nails are made of tempered steel, which are difficult to cut and once they are cut they will have to be ground smooth whether you add a finished wall or not. You can pound the nails into the concrete block wall until they are flush with that wall. The problem here is that the wall will not be airtight or watertight. The best solution is to rent a very large crowbar and remove the nails. Then fill the holes with caulking specially designed for concrete and masonry walls. This will make the wall both airtight and watertight.

**Q** I have dark wood paneling in my basement. I don't want to replace it because it is in good condition, but I find the color too dark. Is there any way I can lighten it?

**A** I always tell people to avoid dark paneling in the basement because most basements have little or no natural light. There are two things you can do. First, you can replace the existing paneling or simply cover it with a new and lighter one. In the last decade, the patterns and colors of panelling have improved immensely. The other possibility is to paint the existing paneling. Paneling is smooth, so you will have to clean with trisodium phosphate and sand the surface lightly first. Then you can apply any type of paint. To avoid sanding, apply a coat of a super adherent primer, followed by any type of paint.

**Q** I recently installed ceramic tiles over the kitchen floor. When they were installed, I was told to never clean the tiled floor with vinegar and water. Several neighbors, who do have a ceramic tiled floor, say they use vinegar and water all the time. Who is right?

**A** Whether you use vinegar and water or a commercial cleaner, neither will damage the tiles themselves. What you must be concerned with is the grout. Vinegar and water—or a stronger cleaner—will hasten the deterioration of the grout. It is also extremely important to apply a silicone sealant over the grout. Without the sealant, the grout will easily absorb water, and within a short period of time that water will damage the wood underneath the tiled floor. Not only will unprotected grout absorb water, but it will also absorb all the dirt that comes with it, and the grout will become discolored and unattractive. Once you apply silicone sealant, keep an eye on it. When you notice the grout is a little discolored, clean the surface and apply another coat of sealant. The frequency with which you have to reapply the sealant will depend on the strength of the cleaner you use.

**Q** I plan to install ceramic tiles in the hallway on the second floor of my house. I have heard conflicting reports about whether I should install them on top of plywood or whether I should install them on top of a mud bed. Which method should I use?

**A** Whether you use plywood or thick set mortar, or "mud bed," there must be a solid floor underneath before you lay ceramic tiles. If you live in an older house, it is likely to have two or three layers of wood underneath. If there are no wood layers underneath, the traditional thick set mortar method may cause the tiles to crack. The thick set mortar method can be more solid, but it requires a certain degree of skill to apply it and a fair amount of time to set properly. If not, you will encounter problems later on. I find that the plywood method is just as effective and much easier to do correctly. It is important to remember that either method will cause the floor level to rise, posing a potential problem with door clearance.

**Q** I want to install ceramic tiles on the concrete floor in my basement. Right now the concrete floor is coated with latex paint. I want to know what is the best way to remove the paint, and what kind of mortar should I put down before placing the tiles?

**A** The easiest and best method for removing paint from concrete is to use a mechanical grinder or a wire brush. This method will guarantee that the surface will be free of any paint. It is a dusty job, so be sure to ventilate the basement well and make sure that you wear a mask. If the floor is not perfectly flat, even it out with a self-leveling concrete mix. For the tile adhesive, my suggestion is that you speak to the professionals at a tile manufacturing center. Each type of tile requires a specific type of mortar, and the tile experts would know which adhesive or mortar works best with your tiles.

**Q** I want to install a grab bar on the wall along my bath-tub. Behind the ceramic tiles are steel studs. Do I have to attach the bar to the steel studs, and if so how do I attach it?

**A** It is difficult to attach a grab bar to ceramic tiles, because they are not strong enough to hold the weight. A metal bolt attached to the steel stud will not hold very well either. This is one of the reasons that I like to install plywood under bathroom ceramic tiles: grab bars can then be securely attached anywhere on the wall. There is a solution to the steel studs, however: toggle bolts or molly bolts can be inserted in holes drilled through the steel stud. Their wings will open up on the other side of the stud, holding the grab bar securely in place. The only problem with this method is lining up the drill with the steel stud. Make sure that you are positive about the location of the steel stud before you begin drilling. Use a drill bit with a carbide-tipped head to drill through the ceramic tile, then switch to a metal drill bit to go through the stud.

**Q** A number of tiles have come loose from the drywall in my bathroom. I want to know how to remove the other ones that are loose without doing too much damage. What is the best method?

**A** The strength of drywall rests with the paper covering either side of the plaster. If the paper is removed from the drywall, you cannot glue the tiles to the surface. Unfortunately, when tiles glued to drywall are removed, often the paper comes off with it. Try removing the tiles gently and you might avoid tearing the drywall paper. If you are unsuccessful, try the following. Once the tiles have been removed, a thin layer of plaster can be added to the wall, and the tiles can be placed on the plaster. Remember that the exposed drywall should be sprayed with water before the plaster is applied. If not, the moisture from the wet plaster will be absorbed by the drywall and the plaster will not adhere properly.

**Q** We have a stand-up shower stall in our basement, and would like to enlarge the shower space to run the entire width of the room. What do we have to do to prepare the floor for tiling?

**A** There are a number of things that have to be done to prepare the floor. A cross section of the floor you need would have a thin layer of cement over the main plywood floor. It is very important that the cement tapers down from where the floor and wall meet to the drain. Over the cement you have to install a waterproof plastic membrane. It should extend from the drain, across the floor, and up the wall 10 cm (4 in.) or so. If a leak later develops on the bottom of the wall, it cannot penetrate beyond the tiles. Above the plastic membrane there should be another thin layer of cement over which the tiles can be set. If you do not want to dig up the floor, you can build the same layers of materials on top of the floor.

**Q** I moved into a new house where there are tiny pinholes in the grout between the tiles around the bathtub. What is the best way to fill the holes, and can I do it without damaging the tiles?

**A** The tiny holes are in the grout because when it was applied, there were tiny bubbles in the grout. There are three items you need to fix this: grout, a silicone sealer, and a small drill bit. Spin the drill bit between your fingers to enlarge the pinholes before filling them with grout. (If you do not enlarge the holes, but simply apply the grout in the existing pinholes, you will have poor results.) Remove any loose material and apply the grout. Clean the surface and then apply the silicone sealer to make the surface waterproof.

**Q** The new floor tiles in our entrance have cracked. What did we do wrong?

**A** Maybe the floor, maybe the adhesive. If the floor is not solid and flexes when you walk on it, ceramic tiles will eventually crack. If the floor is not flat, having ridges where two boards or plywood meet, the tile will crack over the joint. That is why we often cover a floor with a sheet of underlay before laying tiles. Now let's look at the adhesive. Have you ever wondered why all tile adhesive is applied with a notched spatula and not a smooth one? If you try to spread out adhesive with a smooth plaster trowel, you will never get it even, and you will probably use much more adhesive than you need. The notched trowel allows you to apply a very specific amount of adhesive to a floor. Each type of tile requires a certain size and shape of notch, which means you will end up with adhesive lines of a certain volume at precise distances from each other. Even all the strange curves we make doesn't change the quantity of adhesive. When you wiggle or "set" the tile into the adhesive you are assuring that it makes good contact with the tile. But you must also assure that the "depth lugs", those spacers built into the bottom of the tiles, are in contact with the floor. If they are not, the tile may settle later on, and crack.

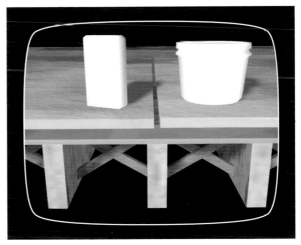

 For more detail, click on "Interiors" on the home screen of the CD-ROM.

55

**Q** I have wall-to-wall carpeting on both the first and second floors of my house. The carpeting is light in color, but is dark and dirty at the edge of the baseboards on the walls facing outside. I know that the problem is not my cleaning or cleaner, so it must be something else. What is it, and what can I do about it?

**A** The problem that you have is air drafts. Directly behind the wall against which your carpet is flush is a 2x4 piece of wood that, over time, has shrunk a little. By shrinking, the wood has opened a small airspace that is allowing in air from the outside. Unfortunately, your carpet is acting as a filter and is collecting dirt, dust, and condensation. The first thing you should do is remove the quarter-round molding at the bottom of the baseboard. Once you pull back the carpeting you will see a space between the edge of the floor and the wall. That space is the culprit. Fill the hole with caulking to seal the space and gently put the carpeting back into place. This simple solution will not cleanse the carpet of its dirt and discoloration, but will immediately stop the problem from continuing.

**Q** I removed a dirty old carpet that was left on the basement floor by the previous owners of my house. Under the carpet was a 6 mm ($^1/_4$ in.) thick rubber underlay. Unfortunately, it has been glued to the floor. What is the easiest method for removing the rubber underlay?

**A** There are two items that will be required to remove the rubber underlay: a heat gun and an old spatula. The heat gun is needed to melt and loosen the glue. Because the glue is under rubber, applying heat to the rubber underlay can be dangerous because of the fumes that it will produce. This is where the old spatula comes in handy. Apply a modest amount of heat to the rubber underlay, enough to loosen the glue slightly, but not enough to melt the rubber. At the same time, push the spatula under the rubber underlay and it will loosen even more. (Sharpening the edge of the spatula can speed up the process.) Once you have removed the rubber underlay, use a sharp scraper to remove the remaining bits of rubber attached to the floor. It will be a slow process, and even with the aid of the spatula and applying only a modest amount of heat, there is still the possibility of danger from fumes. Make sure that the room is properly ventilated and that you wear a mask.

**Q** I removed the carpeting on the inside stairs in a house that I recently bought. The wood underneath the carpeting is softwood. I was told that I cannot varnish soft wood. Is this true, and if so, what can I do to improve the look of the stairs?

**A** The problem with softwood steps is that a good polyurethane finish will be harder than the wood. If enough weight is applied to the step, the finish will crack. It can work, but regular maintenance will be required. You could create "hardwood steps" by covering the existing steps with 6 mm ($1/4$ in.) thick prefinished hardwood floor panels. They can be glued into place over the existing steps. Since every step would be covered, the height of the steps will remain even. The only problem with this project is that you will have to install wood trims on the edge of each step. If you add another layer of wood to the existing steps then two layers of wood will be visible at the step edge. Find a wood trim that matches the new "hardwood" steps to cover the edges.

**Q** There is some wall-to-wall carpeting on the basement floor of my house. The carpeting is glued to the concrete floor underneath. I want to put some new carpeting down. Can I place the new carpet on top of the old, or do I have to first remove the existing carpet?

**A** You can do either, but there are some concerns for both options. If you remove the carpeting, you will have to flatten out the glue on the concrete surface. You do not have to remove it completely, but you will have to scrape it smooth. The benefit of laying the new carpet over the old—aside from saving the trouble of scraping off the glue—is that the old carpet will act as an underlay. But you must be absolutely certain that there is no moisture in or under that carpet. If the room already smells musty, then you should remove the old carpet first. If there is no odor, lift up the edge of the carpet in several places and examine the underside of the carpet. If it is dry and odorless, then proceed with laying down the new carpet over the old.

**Q** I moved into a house whose previous owners had installed wall-to-wall carpeting. I want to keep the carpeting, but there are a number of cigarette burns on it. Is there any way of repairing the sections of the carpet that have the cigarette burns?

**A** There are a couple of things that you can do to repair the carpet. For the burns that are small and minor in damage, pick at the burned section with either a pocket knife or a pair of tweezers. After doing this for a minute or two, the fibers of the carpet sealed under the burned carpet will reappear. If the cigarette burns are larger and too damaged to repair, there is an alternative. If your wall-to-wall carpeting extends into a closet, cut a patch from the carpet there, where no one will notice a small piece missing. First, cut out the section of burned carpeting, making the piece a slightly larger than the burned area. Then cut a patch of the same size from the closet carpet. You can then glue the patch into the section that had the burn. If the carpet has a pattern or design, use the same technique but find some hidden carpet that matches the pattern of the burned area.

**Q** I have heard conflicting stories about whether I should use 12 mm ($^1/_2$ in.) plywood as an underlay for a ceramic tile floor. Is this thick enough?

**A** The first thing that you have to establish is whether the floor onto which you will install the plywood is level. If the floor is level and solid, then 12 mm ($^1/_2$ in.) or even 9 mm ($^3/_8$ in.) plywood will suffice. Once you screw down the plywood, you can then glue on the ceramic tiles and you should not encounter any problems. The reason for this is if the floor is rigid and completely level, the floor will absorb all the weight—not the newly installed plywood. If, however, the floor is not level or flexes too much, and you install the plywood, it will bend here and there, with loose and cracking ceramic tiles the end result. If the hardwood floor beneath is not completely level and solid, you should use 15 mm ($^5/_8$ in.) tongue-and-groove plywood. Before installing it, you should also ensure that the joists below the floor are properly reinforced.

**Q** I installed a linoleum tile floor in my kitchen about six months ago. In that time, the parts of the floor that are exposed to sunlight have become increasingly discolored. Is the sunlight responsible for the discoloration, and what can I do about it?

**A** Bright sunlight will discolor anything, including linoleum floors. If you have applied wax to the linoleum floor, it may be the wax, and not the linoleum, that has become increasingly discolored. In the same way that wax becomes discolored from dirt and traffic, sunlight can deteriorate its surface. What is required is periodic cleaning and rewaxing. Use a strong detergent to clean the floor thoroughly, and then apply a wax specifically designed for linoleum. This should help your immediate problem, but you will have to put in a little elbow grease from time to time.

**Q** I have vinyl flooring in my kitchen that is about seven years old. There are two large pieces with a seam running down the middle of the room, and one piece is lifting up and curling away from the plywood underneath. Is there something that I can do to repair it?

**A** There is little that can be done to repair it permanently. If the vinyl is curling upward, then it is showing its age. Soon after it starts to curl, it is likely to crack also. There is a short-term solution to the problem. You can use an iron on the floor to flatten the curled piece of vinyl, as long as you lay out a towel first. This way the vinyl will absorb the heat and flatten into place, but it will not burn. Once it has been flattened, put some weights or some books over it to ensure that it is flat. While the books are in place, the vinyl can cool at the same time. When it has cooled, put contact cement on both the underside of the vinyl and on the plywood floor. It is important to apply the contact cement on both surfaces, or it will not stick. It is also important not to connect the two surfaces immediately after the contact cement has been applied. Let it dry until it is tacky before pressing the vinyl into place. You are going to have to replace the vinyl within a couple of years, but you will have a flat floor in the meantime.

**Q** When I walk across my bedroom floor, the lamp almost bounces off the night table. Is my floor dangerous and how can I fix it?

**A** Any wood, metal, or even concrete stretched out too far without support will become springy. Although a springy floor may not be in danger of breaking through, there are construction regulations designed to avoid the trampoline effect. Span tables are developed for the building code by the Canadian Wood Council to give acceptable distances between supports for each type of floor assembly. If the supports are too far apart for the size of your floor joists and you cannot simply support them underneath with another beam and posts, you can remove some of the spring from a floor by making it more rigid. Adding or re-nailing cross bracing in-between the joists will help, as will nailing 1x3 strapping across the joists. In new construction, gluing the subfloor to the joists or using a thicker subfloor in addition to bracing will stiffen the floor even more.

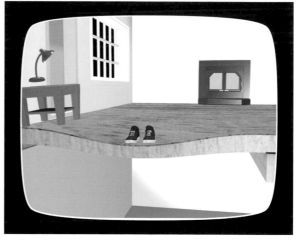

 For more detail, click on "Structure" on the home screen of the CD-ROM.

**Q** There is a gap that has developed between the ceiling and the drywall in my upstairs bedroom. Someone told me that the problem lies with the foundation of the house, but the wall in question is in the middle of the house, and is not an exterior wall. What is causing the problem?

**A** You are correct. The problem is not the foundation, but what is called truss uplift. Some individual trusses, under special circumstances, buckle upward and raise the ceiling. These special circumstances include: high attic humidity, cold weather, part of the truss may be buried in insulation, or specific truss designs. These trusses are safe, but bothersome. You can hide the crack with molding installed 2.5 cm (1 in.) below the ceiling. If you change the drywall, attach the ceiling drywall to the partition wall without any nails on the truss 45 cm (18 in.) from the wall. This allows the ceiling to flex or bend with truss movement without cracking.

**Q** The floor joists under the first floor of my 20-year-old house are warping. Is it possible to repair the problem without replacing the joists?

**A** Yes. First, in the basement, jack the joists up to a level that is slightly above what is considered normal. Line up pieces of 19 mm ($^3/_4$ in.) thick plywood flush with the either side of the warped joists. They must be flush with the joists, but they must also be flush with the plywood flooring above. The best way to attach the pieces of wood to the joists is using screws and construction adhesive. If you decide to use nails, make sure that you hammer in the nails at different angles so that the nails will not pull out due to pressure. If you can, make sure that the pieces of wood installed are the same width as the joists. This will add to their strength. Another thing that can be done to improve the strength of the joists and to prevent curving of the floor is to add blocks between, and perpendicular to, the joists. Once this is completed, the jacks can be removed.

**Q** The floors in our house have always squeaked. We are planning major renovations, so how can we get rid of the squeaks in the floor?

**A** Glue it down! Construction adhesive can solve a lot of common problems. When floors are new, the nails hold the subfloor tight to the joists. But after the wood dries out, there is often a space left between the plywood and the joists. It is the rubbing between these two pieces of wood, and rubbing on the nail, that makes a squeaky floor. Many floors have even more layers of wood and the squeaking can come from any two of these rubbing together. Construction adhesive will go a long way toward preventing squeaking. All the layers of wood stay locked together even if they shrink, and you get a more rigid floor as well. Construction adhesive comes in caulking gun type cartridges. Simply gun a single line of adhesive down the middle of the floor joist before putting down the subfloor. Then use flooring screws, not nails, to attach to the joists. If you are putting down a thin underlay over the plywood, make a snakelike pattern with the adhesive and then screw down the underlay as well.

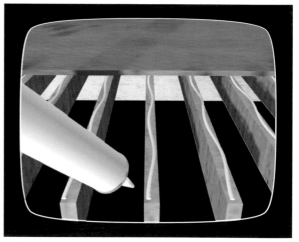

 For more detail, click on "Structure" on the home screen of the **CD-ROM**.

**Q** I live in a semi-detached house that was built in the 1980s. My living room wall, which measures about 2.4 m x 1.8 m (8 ft x 6 ft), is opposite my neighbors' kitchen wall. Even when they are talking quietly in their kitchen I can hear them, and when doors slam or music is played it is even worse. What is the most economical way to soundproof the wall?

**A** Soundproofing is never an easy job. High-frequency sounds move through the air and low-frequency sounds such as slamming doors and bass-heavy music can travel through structures. Party walls that are properly built have what is called resilient bars between the stud wall and the drywall. These are Z-shaped pieces of metal that help muffle sound. If the wall does not have the resilient clips, then you can either tear down the drywall, install resilient bars, and erect a new dry-wall, or install resilient bars on the existing drywall and put up two new layers of drywall over that. Any empty spaces in the wall should be filled with any kind of soft insulation. Also fill any airholes in the wall with standard foam-in-a-can insulation. This will definitely reduce and muffle sound coming from next door. You can also ask your neighbors to do the same thing on their side of the wall.

**Q** The hardwood floors on the ground floor of my house squeak when anyone walks across them. The underside of the floor is exposed in the unfinished base-ment. Is there any way to tackle the problem from the basement?

**A** Let me warn you first that if you do too thorough a job of correcting the problem of squeaky floors, the problem may return because the squeaking was caused by expansion and con-traction. With that in mind, you should only make an effort to fix sections of the floor that are exposed to a lot of traffic and let the rest move. Have someone walk across the effected areas while you touch the same floor from the basement. If you feel the floor move and hear a squeak, gently insert a cedar shim with a small amount of glue between the floor and the joist. If you cannot feel any movement, the problem is between the subfloor and the hardwood. Screws from below can pull the hardwood down securely.

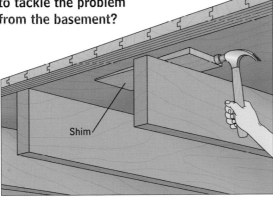

Shim

**Q** I recently had a small flood in my basement. I pulled up the parquet floor to limit the damage to the wood. I have solved the flooding and dried the floor completely. Is there any special way of reinstalling the parquet floor?

**A** It is imperative that the floor be completely dry before you put the flooring back in place. Once you are certain of this, you can proceed and replace the wood. However, if the parquet floor was exposed to any water it is likely that some minor damage occurred. Check that the floor has not swollen and that it will lie in an even pattern. If necessary, trim the edges with a table saw. You should have to sand and revarnish the floor only if it is not smooth and even.

**Q** I have some parquet floors that are covered with wax. I want to remove the wax and varnish the wood. What is the best method for removing the wax, and is any preparation for the floor required before the varnish is added?

**A** Wax removers are available at hardware stores. They are solvents that break down the wax and make it easier to remove. Remember that the wax has to be picked up and removed. If you apply the solvent and push a mop across the floor, you will have accomplished nothing other than spreading the wax on the floor. It must be picked up. Once the wax has been removed, lightly sand the wood with very fine sandpaper just to remove the gloss of the old varnish. This will give some bite to the floor and allow the varnish to adhere well without damaging the wood.

**Q** We moved into a house where the floors are covered in varnish, shellac, or varathane. We do not know which was applied, but some of it is now flaking off. How can we find out which one was applied, and what can be done to repair the floors?

**A** Apply to the floor some old fingernail polish remover that contains acetone. If it dissolves, then you have old varnish on the floor. If it does not dissolve, then the floor is covered in varathane or urethane. If it is varathane or urethane you will have to use sandpaper or paint stripper to get it off. If it is varnish, you can apply a furniture restorer to it without having to first strip it off. The restorer will dissolve the existing varnish and cover it nicely.

**Q** I live in a four-story split-level house. On the third floor the family room, office, and bathroom have wood ceilings and trim. I don't think the wood has ever been treated, but I would like to protect it. I'm most concerned about the wood in the bathroom because it has only a small window for ventilation. What can I apply to the wood to protect it?

**A** The first thing that you have to do is install an exhaust fan. Nothing will eliminate the humidity in a small room more effectively. If you are concerned about the noise an exhaust fan will produce, there are exhaust fans on the market that are so quiet that the on/off light is the only indicator that it is operating. You can further protect the wood ceiling and trim by treating it. You can apply a glossy or matte varnish, which is very safe to do inside. These finishes work well in a bathroom because they are resistant to humidity and fungus. You can also apply oil to the wood. However, the problem with applying oil is that it becomes dirty very quickly. You will find the best results with varnish and, of course, installing an exhaust fan.

# PLUMBING

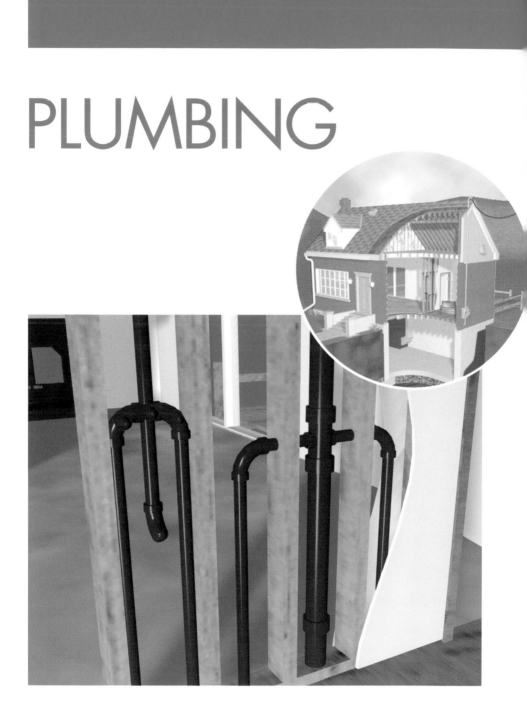

# CHAPTER 3

We have certainly come a long way since the days of outdoor plumbing, and I don't think that any of us want to go back. Think for a moment just what all those pipes do.

Water arrives in the house under tremendous pressure, pressure that has to be controlled at all times or we get plumbing floods. We then split part of it off and heat it, thus requiring two input systems throughout the house: cold and hot. Now we want faucets that give us hot or cold or some nice controlled combination of the two—and we don't want that to fluctuate, especially while we are in the shower.

Then we want all that water to simply flow out of the house, taking with it any junk we want to send, from laundry soap to toilet waste to garborated garbage. Of course we don't want the drain to clog, we don't want any of those outhouse odors coming back into the house, and we would prefer it to do all of this quietly.

But the convenience of indoor plumbing has made life at times complicated if not mysterious. We understand faucets and drains, but few understand the vent system that allows the drains to work properly and most of this is hidden inside the walls. Here are some of the plumbing mysteries that I have tried to help you to investigate.

**Q** My tap water tastes terrible. Will a commercial water filter do me any good?

**A** Yes, but you need to choose the right one for the composition of your water and what you want to accomplish. Basically, municipal water in Canada is quite safe to drink. The problem is that your water can contain things that do not affect safety but affect taste, like chlorine—which is often used to rid water of harmful bacteria but tastes terrible—or sulfur. There can also be elements present that make it difficult to wash clothes or keep the sink clean, like calcium or iron. Some water purification systems, like reverse osmosis, can do a great job under certain circumstances, but would get all clogged up if you have a lot of iron in your water. Even distilled water is not pure $H_2O$ because chlorine tends to evaporate with the boiling process and carry right over into the condensed steam, requiring filtering through activated charcoal to clean up the taste. Filters are available for the end of faucet spigots or the shower head, or you can buy a larger countertop purification unit. However, the most effective water purification will be with larger units installed right on the water lines because they can handle more water for a longer time. Have your water tested to know what is in it and then get a professional who sells more than one model to help you to choose.

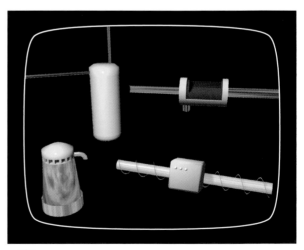

 For more detail, click on "Plumbing" on the home screen of the **CD-ROM.**

**Q** I live in a 60-year-old house where the water pressure is quite low. All the piping in the interior of the house is copper, with the exception of a 2.7 m (9 ft) long pipe leading from the street into the house and the main valve. How can I tell if the water pressure problem is due to the copper pipes in my house or if the problem lies with the city's pipe entering my house?

**A** If you have a faucet beside or close to the main valve, turn it on and see what the pressure is like there. If the pressure is strong, but weak elsewhere in the house, then the problem lies with the piping inside your house. You will have to investigate, but I gather that it is probably a case of a slow blockage somewhere within the piping system. If the pressure is weak right beside the main valve, then the problem lies with the city piping. If this is the case, then you should contact the city and tell them. Another possibility is that the main valve itself is the problem. Try turning the valve off completely and then turning it on again. Sometimes the main valve needs to be tinkered with in order to have full water pressure.

**Q** There are so many different types of pipes. What are their differences?

**A** If you have galvanized steel pipes in your house, then you know the house is old. They were the standard pipes used in homes for almost a century until the use of copper piping by contractors became the standard in the 1960s and 1970s. Copper was popular because it was easy to cut, was lighter than galvanized steel pipes, and unlike galvanized steel pipes, did not rust and corrode. The most popular pipes today are made of plastic. They are even lighter than copper, are less expensive, and easier to cut. Plastic pipes come in a wide variety with a number of differences. The general rule is that polyvinyl chloride pipes and acrylonitrile butadiene styrene pipes, which are resistant to chemicals, are used for drain lines. Chlorinated polyvinyl chloride pipes are used primarily for hot and cold water supply lines.

**Q** I installed a new faucet in my bathroom about a year ago. The faucet is the type that moves up and down to increase and decrease pressure, and left and right to change temperature. The tap has been giving me trouble lately, being extremely stiff and difficult to move. What is the problem?

**A** You are having one of two problems. These faucets have a cartridge that slides inside a cylinder. Something in the water may have dissolved the existing lubrication. Open the cylinder and apply some vaseline. The other possibility is that if your water supply is rich in iron, there may be a buildup of the metal inside the faucet system. You can tell if this is happening because water exiting the faucet will have a red tint to it. If this is the case, correcting the problem is simple enough. The cartridge inside the faucet needs to be replaced and the cylinder in which it slides should be rubbed with some steel wool. It is not very expensive and if you are worried about having the right part after you have left the hardware store, take the cartridge that you have into the store with you.

**Q** Every time I turn on the hot water faucet for my bathroom sink, it rattles, vibrates, and makes a lot of noise. What is causing this, and how can I correct it?

**A** This is one problem that is very annoying, but also very simple and inexpensive to fix. One of two things is happening to make the faucet vibrate. If there is an O-ring halfway down the stem, and it is old, the stem may wobble back and forth, causing the vibration. The other possibility is that the seat washer may be loose. If so, it may vibrate up and down. Both should be replaced.

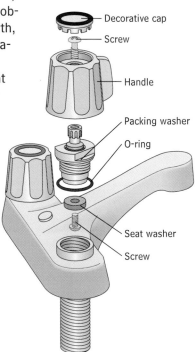

Decorative cap

Screw

Handle

Packing washer

O-ring

Seat washer

Screw

**Q** I can never get a sink plunger to clean out the clogs in my sink. What am I doing wrong?

**A** Unplugging a clogged sink with a plunger is easy, once you understand the principle behind how a plunger works. Pumping up and down does no good if you don't block the overflow because all the pressure from the plunger just moves up the double wall of the sink and out the overflow. No pressure is put on the clog. Stuff a rag into the overflow and hold it there with one hand. Now the second secret is that the plunger pushes water to the side in the down stroke, which doesn't put much pressure on the blockage. In fact, putting pressure on a blockage might make it block even more. The key is the up-stroke. On the way up, the plunger creates a good suction under the cup, pulling the blockage back into the sink.
A blockage will have less resistance to coming back than to going forward. That will break up the blockage and everything can flow away.

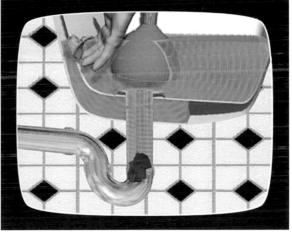

 For more detail, click on "Plumbing" on the home screen of the **CD-ROM.**

**Q** I live alone in a two-story house. Everyday, when I return from work in the evening, the level of water in the toilet bowl on the first floor has dropped at least 5 cm (2 in.). What could the problem be?

**A** The first possibility is that the porcelain underneath is cracked. The loss of that much water a day is not a lot if there is a leak. A crack in the porcelain could result in a relatively slow leak. The other possibility is that there is an elongated strand of human hair or dental floss hung up in the drain. If half of the strands are sitting in the drain pipe leading from the toilet, and the other half are hanging inside the toilet bowl, but out of view, then the 5 cm (2 in.) of water loss during the day is likely to be the result of the string siphoning the water into the drain pipe. You should not have a problem with pulling the string out because your toilet is flushing well to begin with. There is not a major blockage, but just that piece of string that is locked in place. Using a simple closet auger may do the trick. If that does not work, then you will have to remove the toilet, turn it upside down, and remove the strands that way.

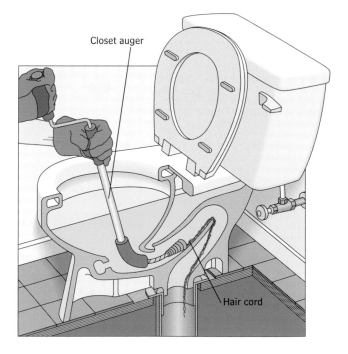

Closet auger

Hair cord

**Q** I would like to install a toilet in my basement. Unfortunately, there is no exposed plumbing in the basement. What should I do to connect the toilet pipes to the house piping system?

**A** The reason that many houses do not have a toilet in the basement is due to the lack of space underneath the basement floor. Toilets require space underneath to allow the drain to slope downward to the sewer drain. Most basements have a cement or concrete floor which means that you will have to dig up the floor to add the piping. If there is a lot of head space in the basement—and there usually isn't—you could install the toilet on an elevated surface. This way the toilet will have the space underneath required, and there will not be a need to dig up the concrete floor. A third option is to install a product called a low-bore toilet. It operates like a normal toilet, but with one difference: attached to the toilet is a garbage disposal-type of unit that pumps the liquefied waste up high enough to easily flow down to the main plumbing stack.

**Q** How do I retrieve a toilet paper roll that was accidentally flushed down the toilet?

**A** There is always the possibility that a toilet auger will not be able to grab onto the paper carton. I would try using the auger first *(see illustration at left)* but if you are unsuccessful, you have to tackle the problem from the other end. You have to turn off and disconnect the water supply and empty the toilet tank of as much water as possible. Once you have done this, remove the screws that hold the toilet to the floor. You can then turn the toilet upside down or turn it on its side. Run the auger from the floor side of the toilet to push the carton back into the bowl. I highly recommend that two people do this job because the toilet is fairly heavy. You do not want to drop it and break it, nor do you want to hurt your back. Remember to replace the wax or foam seal ring when replacing the toilet.

**Q** Every time I turn on the bathtub faucet rusty, orange-brown water comes out. I'm not sure if the problem is with the water itself or with the pipes. What is causing it and what can I do about it?

**A** If this occurs only when you turn on the hot-water faucet, it may be due to an accumulation of sludge in your hot water tank. You can fix this by flushing the tank with water. Add a hose to the spigot at the bottom of the tank and run it

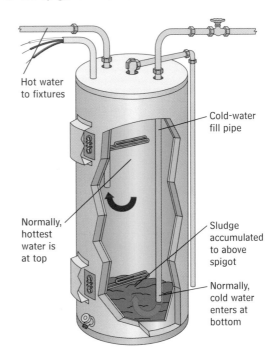

Hot water to fixtures

Cold-water fill pipe

Normally, hottest water is at top

Sludge accumulated to above spigot

Normally, cold water enters at bottom

to the floor drain. Run water from the tank until the water turns clear. Homeowners are recommended to perform this task annually. If the rusty water is coming out of the cold-water faucet, it is coming from galvanized steel pipes. The pipes have rusted on the inside and the rust is being carried through the pipes every time you turn on the faucet. There are two possible solutions to this problem. The first is to replace the pipes. If the galvanized steel pipes are part of the piping system within your house, you can replace them with copper pipes. If the affected pipes run from the house to the street, however, then a major digging operation will be necessary. The second, easier, solution is to add phosphate crystals to a filter unit that is installed just after the main water valve. Over time the crystals form a coating on the inside of the pipes that hold the rust in place.

**Q** What kind of paint should I use to remove rusty discoloration marks on the bottom of my bathtub?

**A** If the porcelain on your bathtub is not chipped but merely discolored, you can probably get rid of the discoloration with a commercial cleaner. If the stain is stubborn, get some oxalic acid from your drugstore. If, however, the porcelain is chipped, there is no paint available that will do the job properly, as it is almost impossible to successfully apply paint to the surface of a bathtub. It will look good for several months, but after that the paint will begin to chip and decay. Professionals can refinish the bathtub with special coatings, but they are expensive. If your bathtub is an old tub that sits on four legs, it can be removed by a professional and taken to their shop. There they will grind off the old enamel and apply a new coating. If your bathtub is attached into the wall, then removing it will create more problems than it is worth.

**Q** Every time I turn off the shower faucet, the water continues to drip down for several minutes. I have made sure that I turn off the faucet tightly and I have changed the washers inside the faucets but the problem persists. What can I do to eliminate the drip?

**A** If you have replaced the washer then obviously the problem lies elsewhere. My guess is that the valve seat—found inside the faucet valves, against which the washer lies—is the culprit. Over time, the valve seat can develop small ridges. Water is thus not being sealed inside the valve and that is what is causing the water to drip. The way to solve the problem is to buy a dresser, a small grinder that can be inserted into the valve. The tip of the dresser, when turned like a screwdriver, will smooth the surface of the valve seat and remove any ridges. Once it has been smoothed, a new washer will complete the job. If the valve seat is actually cracked, then it will have to be replaced. Buy an inexpensive valve seat wrench, valve seat, and washer for this job at the hardware or plumbing store.

**Q** When the dish-washer and washing machine are running, or someone flushes the toilet, water pressure in the shower becomes weak and the temperature changes. I have 12 mm ($^1/_2$ in.) copper piping. If I changed it to 19 mm ($^3/_4$ in.) piping, would my water pressure improve?

**A** I would not change all the piping in the house to 19 mm ($^3/_4$ in.). That is too big. What you can do is change the piping that leads to the shower to 19 mm ($^3/_4$ in.), and leave the rest as is. Less work will be required and when you are in the shower the larger pipe will give the shower priority. The temperature will continue to change when the other machines are activated, but not nearly as much. Better yet, you could install a pressure balancing shower faucet that automatically adjusts to keep the temperature constant even if the water pressure fluctuates. The volume of water in the shower will change—but the temperature will remain constant. If you do both these things, the larger piping will give you more pressure, and the pressure-balancing valve will protect you from shower shock.

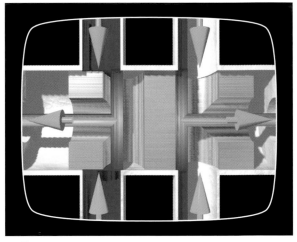

 For more detail, click on "Plumbing" on the home screen of the **CD-ROM.**

**Q** The flow of water from my shower head is uneven. Can the problem be corrected without installing a new shower head?

**A** The distribution of water from the shower head is erratic because there is a calcium buildup in the grooves of the shower head. There are two things that can be done to return proper flow of water through the shower head. Unscrew and dismantle the shower head. Remove the calcium with a small penknife or a toothpick. The other way is to place a small plastic bag filled with a few ounces of vinegar over the shower head. Hold the bag in place with a rubber band and let the vinegar soak into the shower head overnight. It is best to have the shower head submerged in the vinegar. Flush the shower head thoroughly the next morning.

**Q** We installed a stand-up shower in our second-floor bathroom about a year ago. Every time someone takes a shower, though, water leaks through the ceiling on the first floor. Where does the problem lie, and what can we do about it?

**A** The problem lies with either the shower floor and walls or the piping. To isolate the problem, flood the shower with a garden hose or a garden sprinkler. If it does not leak, then the problem is with the faucets or shower head. You will have to open up the wall behind the shower and check the supply piping. The problem is usually between the faucets and the shower head, so open the wall closer to the shower head. If it does leak, isolate its location. Allow the area to dry, then carefully run water down the drain, without touching the floor. If it leaks, you will know that it is the drain pipe. If you have determined that it is not the drain pipe, use the same test covering the floor of the shower with water. If it leaks, the problem is the joint between the tiles and drain.

**Q** I am going to install a new sink in my basement. I will have to add an extension of copper piping to the water supply. Is soldering the piping joints together a do-it-yourself job, or do I need a professional to do it?

**A** Yes, this is a do-it-yourself job. Aside from the copper piping, you will need some steel wool or fine emery cloth, a pipe-burnishing brush, flux, solder and a propane blowtorch. Clean both parts of the piping that will be joined with the steel wool or emery cloth. You can clean out the inside of the larger pipe with the pipe-burnishing brush. Before joining the two pieces together generously rub flux on both pieces. Flux is designed to oxidize the copper and help pull the solder into the pipe and make the connection more secure. If you do not use flux, future leaks are guaranteed. When soldering the two pieces of copper together do not make the mistake of melting the solder with the blowtorch. The blowtorch should be used only to increase the heat of the copper. Once it is hot enough, the solder will easily melt when touched to the surface of the pipes. If the piping is close to a wall make sure the wall is protected by a heat pad, and remember to wear safety goggles.

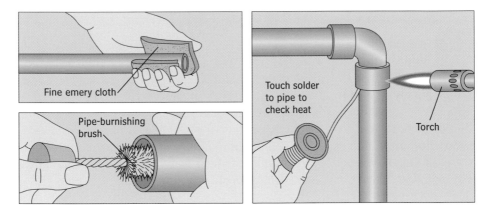

Fine emery cloth

Pipe-burnishing brush

Touch solder to pipe to check heat

Torch

**Q** I have been experiencing problems with the stack pipe, which passes through an unheated garage. During the winter the stack freezes. Why is it a problem, and what can I do about it?

**A** The natural assumption on how to insulate pipes in cold spaces is to wrap insulation around them completely. That, however, is a mistake. If you wrap your stack pipe in insulation, it will keep the cold air away from the stack, but it will also prevent exposure to heat from the interior of the house, which is what it needs. If the stack is running through the unprotected garage, that is likely where it is freezing. What you want to do is box in the stack system so that it is being protected from cold on one side, but exposed to the warmth of the house on the other side. Build a wall on the side of the stack that is facing the garage. It does not have to be an elaborate wall, but just a barrier of some kind. Then you should put insulation between that wall and the stack, but leave the house side of the stack uninsulated. By doing this, the cold air from the garage will be stopped by the wall and the insulation, and the exposed side of the stack will receive heat from the house. Even if there is a solid wall blocking the way, the heat will get through. If the stack is insulated on both sides, that heat will not penetrate the insulation.

**Q** I am planning to renovate my bathroom. I would like to install a sink and a shower on one side of the wall and a washer and dryer on the other side of the wall. Is it possible to connect all the drain pipes and vent pipes together?

**A** Yes. There should not be any problem with connecting all the pipes to the same drainage system. The function of the vent system is to provide free air to the drain pipe to prevent the suction of flowing water from draining the traps. Its other function, of course, is to prevent foul pipe odors from entering the house. If the position of the washing machine on the other side of the wall is too far from the main vent pipes, a simple solution can be found. A vent valve can be installed which will open up and draw in air when the pipe is flushed. Once the water has passed, the damper will close and prevent any foul air from moving through the water pipe. The valve rises only 10 cm (4 in.) or so above the pipe and eliminates the need to attach long vent piping. Remember that vent valves are not permitted on toilet drains.

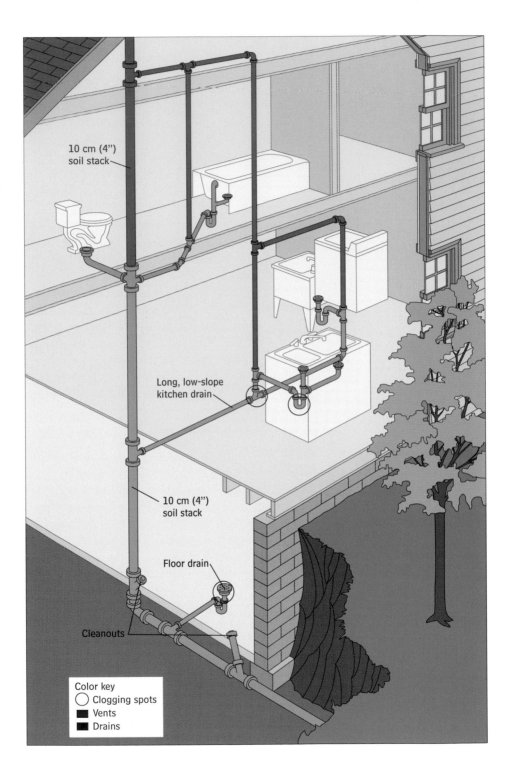

10 cm (4")
soil stack

Long, low-slope
kitchen drain

10 cm (4")
soil stack

Floor drain

Cleanouts

Color key
○ Clogging spots
▪ Vents
▪ Drains

**Q** My main drain leading from the roof to the basement passes through the wall that separates the kitchen and the living room. When the toilet is flushed, or the shower is running in the second-floor bathroom the falling water makes a lot of noise. Is there anything that I can do to reduce or eliminate the sound?

**A** When drains work properly, water swirls around the edges of the main drain pipe on the way to the basement, rather than falling down the middle. When it does fall down the middle it makes a lot of noise. Most new houses have plastic pipes that are less effective at muffling the sound than old cast-iron pipes. The only solution I have is to open the wall and fill the cavity around the plumbing stack with fiberglass to muffle the sound. If you are lucky enough to have the pipe run alongside a closet wall, go in through the closet to minimize the wall repair job.

**Q** For several minutes after I flush the toilet I can hear a dripping noise. I am not sure whether the dripping is coming from inside the pipes or if there is water leaking outside the pipes. What is causing it and what can I do about it?

**A** The toilet drain runs across the room from the toilet to the plumbing stack on a slight slope. Sometimes things accumulate in the pipe that do not flush away, particularly if the house has settled and the slope of the pipe has evened itself. The worst culprit is long human hair, usually from cleaning hair brushes and throwing the hair in the toilet, or discarded dental floss. These long fibrous materials can stick to the walls of the pipe where it joins the vent stack and hangs over the edge of the vertical stack. They do not block the toilet, but the last bit of water that comes lazily down the horizontal pipe slowly and noisily drips off the ends of the hair or floss into the stack pipe. If you can't live with the dripping, it will be necessary to clear the drain line to the plumbing stack. This usually requires removal of the toilet from the floor to gain access to the floor opening.

**Q** There are two sinks in my basement, both with one spout and two valves. Every time I turn on the hot water, only cold water comes out. The problem does not exist anywhere else in the house. I have been unable to investigate the pipes because there is no shutoff valve for the two sinks. What is the problem?

**A** My first impression is that someone did a bad plumbing job and that only the cold water source was connected to the two sinks. To test this, turn off the water at the hot water tank. Test it upstairs by opening the hot water faucet. If nothing comes out, then the valve is safely closed. Now turn on the hot water in those basement sinks. If water comes out, the hot water is not even piped into the faucets, and the cold water is pumped into both sides. If this is the case you are going to have to locate the nearest hot water lead and pipe it to the sinks. While you are at it, you should install shutoff valves on each feed under the sinks.

**Q** We installed a shower in our basement about one year ago. We have noticed a gaseous odor emanating from the drain. What can we do to eliminate the odor?

**A** Perhaps you never installed a trap under this shower, and sewer gases are moving up the drain. If you did install a trap, but use the shower irregularly, the water in the trap may evaporate and let through the gases. Pour a pitcher of water into the drain. If the odor goes away after a day or two, the problem is evaporation. Run water into this drain regularly. The problem may also lie in the vent system. Have someone open a few faucets upstairs and flush a toilet or two, while you carefully listen to the shower drain in the basement. If you hear a gurgling sound and can still smell odors, then the vent pipe is not working properly. This pipe prevents water flow from sucking water out of the shower trap. Make sure that there is an air vent on the drain line immediately after the trap. This is either a PVC pipe that goes up and into the vent stack, or a simple "vent valve" that is very useful when a vent is difficult to install.

**Q** Is there any way that I can secure a shower head that moves from the wall when it is touched? Will all that rattling make it burst?

**A** This is a common problem that occurs over time. The combination of human touch and pipe movement when water is flowing through them often causes the pipes to spring loose from their attachment inside the wall. There is no great danger of the pipe bursting, but it can be annoying, sometimes unsightly, and—if the pipe leading to the shower head shakes when it is being turned on or off—it can be noisy. Often there is little space to work with. Usually not enough to see inside, let alone enough to insert a screwdriver or a hammer. There is, however, a simple solution. Push the shower head back into the wall as far as it will go. Tape the shower head against the wall so that it will not move. Fill the hole with foam-in-a-can insulation. (Be careful not to fill the hole in the wall completely because the foam will expand.) Once it has hardened, the shower head will not move.

**Q** I have a frozen steel pipe in my basement. I there anything I can do to thaw it before the pipe bursts?

**A** Yes, there is. Close the shutoff valve and turn on the faucet that leads to the frozen pipe. After wrapping rags around the pipe, pour a pot of boiling water on the rags. It may take several pots, but the pipe will eventually thaw. The same process can be used with a hair dryer instead of boiling water. It is very important to begin either method on the section of pipe that is closest to the faucet, moving further away from the faucet as the ice thaws. The reason for this is because a buildup of pressure can occur as the pipe thaws. If the pressure is not able to escape the pipe will burst. The faucet is the only outlet for the pressure to escape, so it is important to keep it clear. To prevent future freezing, you should insulate your pipes.

**Q** When it rains, water seeps up through my basement floor. Last year I had the property landscaped, so I know that that is not the problem. What could it be?

**A** If landscaping did not solve the problem, then it sounds as if the water table under your house is naturally high. Even if the amount of water entering the basement is minor, it is still going to drastically raise the humidity level in the basement. The only way to solve this problem is to install a sump pump. It will turn on automatically when the water enters the basement. This will reduce the long-term damage to the floor itself, and more importantly it will keep the humidity level of the basement, and the entire house, down.

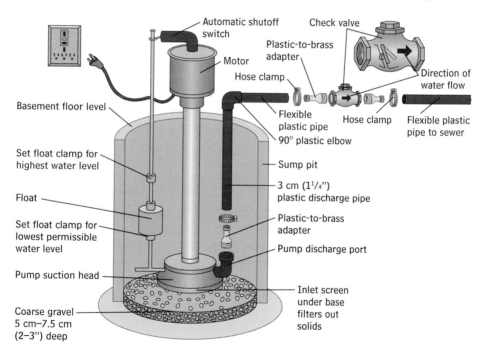

Automatic shutoff switch

Check valve

Plastic-to-brass adapter

Motor

Hose clamp

Direction of water flow

Basement floor level

Flexible plastic pipe

Hose clamp

Flexible plastic pipe to sewer

90° plastic elbow

Set float clamp for highest water level

Sump pit

3 cm (1¼") plastic discharge pipe

Float

Set float clamp for lowest permissible water level

Plastic-to-brass adapter

Pump discharge port

Pump suction head

Inlet screen under base filters out solids

Coarse gravel 5 cm–7.5 cm (2–3") deep

**Q** I recently removed an old sump pump, and filled the hole in the floor that it had created with foam and cement because of a mild, but offensive odor emanating from the hole. Yet the odor remains. What is the problem?

**A** If you filled the hole with cement, then the odor is not coming from there. To find out, open a large plastic garbage bag and place it over the cemented area. Tape the edges of the bag to the ground and wait 24 hours. Open the bag and smell it. If the odor is coming from there, then it was obviously not sealed properly. The best thing to do is dig up the cement and redo it. It is more likely that the odor is coming from some source of condensation in the basement. Water pipes that run inside the wall often develop condensation that can carry odors. Concrete covered with insulation that is not properly sealed is also a common source of basement odors. Insulate water pipes against summer condensation, use vapor barriers on insulated walls, and seal electrical outlets airtight.

**Q** For several weeks I have noticed a foul odor coming from the bathroom sink when I turn on the hot water. Is there something wrong with the water supply, or is there a problem with the piping?

**A** If the odor is emanating from only one sink, then the problem is not with the water supply. It is most likely a small buildup of hair, lint, and dirt caught in between the spillover and the sink drain. The buildup attracts bacteria that carry a bad odor. To correct the problem, you must block the drain below the point where the spillover meets the drain, about 5 cm (2 in.) down the drain. Once it is blocked with a rag or small towel, fill the rest of the drain with a 50/50 mixture of water and bleach. As you fill the drain, it will enter the spillover. Leave it there for an hour and the bacteria will be killed and the odor will disappear. If the odor is coming from all hot water faucets in the house, then the problem likely lies with sediment buildup in the hot water tank. If drained every year, the hot water tank should not create any foul smelling water.

# LIGHTING & ELECTRICITY

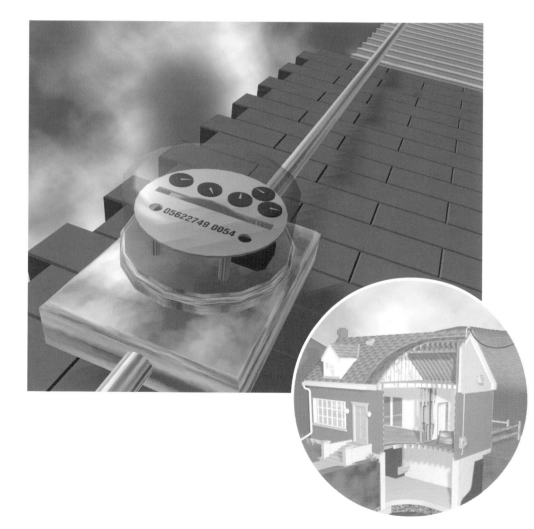

# CHAPTER 4

We all know that we need to be careful with electricity, but in Canada some provinces are more careful than others. The components of your house's entire electrical system—from fuses to the main circuit breaker—can be purchased at hardware stores in every province, yet some provinces forbid anyone other than a licensed electrician to install them. Most provinces do permit major electrical work to be done by homeowners, however, as long as they obtain the proper permits.

As this chapter demonstrates, you don't need a permit to replace an outlet. You can safely undertake many small electrical maintenance tasks yourself, provided you take the simple precautions of removing fuses or turning off circuit breakers before starting. Also, carefully think things through thoroughly before wiring. Take written notes as to which wire was attached to which screw before removing them. Or tag each wire with a note or a number to help keep things straight. Above all, never work with electricity alone. In case something goes wrong, it is good to have somebody else around. Besides, it saves you a lot of running back and forth to the circuit breaker box.

**Q** I need to replace an electric receptacle in my living room. What precautions should I take before changing a receptacle?

**A** None, other than turning off the circuit breaker before you start working. After taking off the cover, unscrew the fixture. There will be mess of wires behind the receptacle. The different colored wires are attached to specifically colored screws. The grounding wire should be attached to the green screw, the black (hot) wire to the brass screw, and the white (neutral) wire to the silver screw. Make sure that they are properly connected before mounting the receptacle back into place and turning the circuit breaker on again.

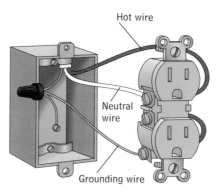

Hot wire

Neutral wire

Grounding wire

**Q** A neighbor has suggested that I replace the existing electrical outlets in my house with something called ground fault circuit interrupters. Should I change them?

**A** Also known as GFCIs, ground fault circuit interrupters are designed to cut off electrical power when a frayed section of live wire is exposed to moisture. GFCIs can be expensive, so if you are going to replace only some of your house's electrical outlets with GFCIs, make sure they are located in areas that have high moisture levels. Kitchens, bathrooms, and crawl spaces are ideal candidates for GFCIs, as well as any outlets found outside your house. Be sure to test ground fault circuit interrupters every month.

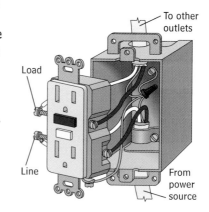

To other outlets

Load

Line

From power source

**Q** I recently bought an older house. This past winter I noticed a draft coming from some of the electrical outlets found along the bottom of the walls. Why is there cold air coming from the boxes and what can I do to correct the problem?

**A** Electrical outlets that appear to be almost flush with the wall actually extend into a hole in the wall and are held in place by an electrical box. Most houses have an air or vapor barrier that is designed to stop drafts through the walls, but most electrical outlets make large holes through this barrier. You have several alternatives. You could seal off the old boxes and run the wiring forward to surface-mounted boxes, thus eliminating the need for the holes. Foam gaskets under the face plate would also help. For a neater solution, you can install polyethylene envelopes around the electrical boxes before nailing them to the studs. This "polypan"—used in new construction or major renovations—is then sealed to the vapor barrier. New construction also uses airtight electrical boxes. The 100 percent seal is made with airtight rubber box inserts that slide into the existing box.

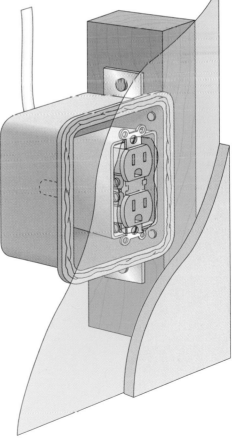

**Q** I want to install a dimmer switch in my dining room. Do I need help installing it or can I do it myself?

**A** It is very easy to install a dimmer switch as long as the process is completed in the proper order. The first thing that you must do is pull out the fuse or turn off the circuit breaker that corresponds to the dining room. Remove the light switch box by disassembling the black and white wires from the screws on the box. Then connect the two wires from the dimmer switch to the two inside the wall. It does not matter if the wires connected to the dimmer switch do not match in color to the wires in the wall. Make sure that the wires are covered with plastic connectors, attach the dimmer switch to the wall and the job is done.

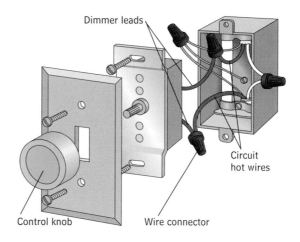

Dimmer leads

Circuit hot wires

Control knob

Wire connector

**Q** I have moved into a new apartment that does not have a light fixture on the ceiling. How am I going to install my ceiling fan?

**A** You will have to buy a shallow surface-mounted junction box that screws into the ceiling. Make sure that it attaches to a stud or a rafter in the ceiling. If not, the fan will tumble to the ground. If you are unable to run any wiring from the space above through the ceiling, run surface wiring with a protective metal covering along the ceiling and down the wall to an outlet.

**Q** I have tried unsuccessfully to install a ceiling fan in my living room. What is the proper method for installing one?

**A** Installing a ceiling fan sometimes seems more difficult than it actually is. The first thing to do is attach the paddle blades to the fan. People often assemble them after they have attached the wires to the light fixture and discover the resulting process a difficult one. Turn off the

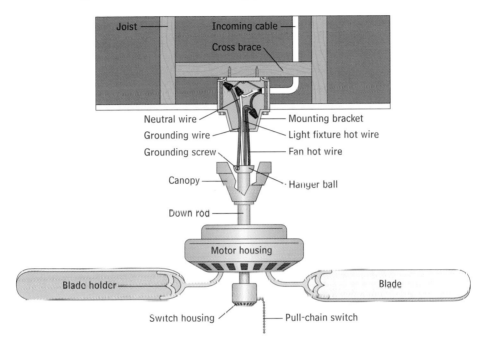

circuit breaker or fuse for the light fixture and then remove the light from the bracket. Usually a large hook comes with the ceiling fan. It attaches to the bracket and allows the ceiling fan to hang while you attach the wiring. Without the hook you would have to hold the fairly heavy ceiling fan with one hand and attach the wires with the other hand. There should be three wires exiting from the fixture: white, red, and black. There should be four wires exiting from the top of the fan; white, green, black, and blue. Both white wires are neutral and should be connected. The fan's grounding wire is green and should be attached to the red wire from the fixture. The fan's black and blue wires are the fan and light wires respectfully. Both should be attached to the black wire from the fixture. Once all the wires are attached, the fan can be screwed into the bracket of the ceiling fixture.

**Q** I want to install some recessed lighting in the ceiling above my bedroom. The room above the bedroom is an insulated attic. I know that I will need a junction box but is the size of the opening important? What else should I look out for?

**A** The size of the opening should fit tightly to the light fixture casing, but the real issue is what type of recessed light fixture you install. There should be an airtight barrier designed to prevent moisture from the house from flowing into the cold attic and causing condensation problems. Some recessed light fixtures will overheat if you insulate them, and most recessed light fixtures leak tremendous quantities of air into the attic—enough to potentially rot out your roof. For years I have recommended not using recessed light fixtures in an insulated attic; track lighting is a better option. But there are new airtight recessed light fixtures specifically designed to be buried in insulation and the casing has no holes in the inner wall. To make the job complete, we come back to your original question, the size of the opening. Cut it tight to the casing and then use the special air-sealing gasket that comes with the airtight fixtures to seal the inner casing to the drywall, closing out all air leakage into the attic. As for the junction box, most electrical codes require that junction boxes be accessible. Accessible from the attic is adequate, and the recessed lights come with a junction box built in.

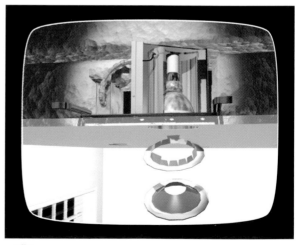

 For more detail, click on "Electricity" on the home screen of the **CD-ROM.**

**Q** Are there any precautions necessary when mounting track lighting?

**A** Track lighting is relatively easy to install and can provide a wide variety of lighting possibilities. If you plan to install lighting that plugs directly into an electrical outlet, your only concern should be that the wire is not too close, or touching, the track lighting. When installing permanently mounted lights, make sure that the power has been cut off, either at the circuit breaker or fuse box, before you start. It would be preferable to screw the track into a ceiling beam, if it is ideally located. If it is not convenient to attach it to a ceiling beam, it is not the end of the world. Most track lights are light enough that they can be held in place using a toggle bolt. The wiring for track lighting is standard and easy to install.

**Q** Is it absolutely necessary to plug in my computer and other appliances to a surge protector?

**A** It is not absolutely necessary, but it is a good idea. Power surges are sudden and sharp changes in circuit voltage. They sometimes occur because of lightning storms, static electricity, and electric motors being turned on and off. Computers, microwave ovens, VCRs, and other modern household appliances are sensitive to power surges, and if exposed to them, can be damaged. Some surges can entirely wipe out the data on the hard drive of a computer. A surge protector senses and absorbs high-voltage surges before they can damage anything that is plugged into an electrical outlet. Surge protectors are inexpensive and will prevent damage to household appliances. Because most surge protectors can accommodate several plugs, they also solve a recurring problem found in many of today's living and work spaces: a lack of outlets.

# HEATING & COOLING

# CHAPTER 5

It is often said that most of Canada has two seasons—a long, cold winter and a short, hot summer. Luckily, almost everything we do for energy conservation in the winter can help to reduce air conditioning costs in the summer.

But our extreme winters do require that we pay close attention to details. A little moisture into the attic and we have condensation. A little heat under the roof and we get ice dams. Change one thing in the house and other things in the system are affected. So it is critically important how we seal holes in the walls as well as how we apply insulation. Chimneys are fine tuned to match their furnaces and should always be considered together as a team. Air flow in and out of the house can take strange paths and needs to be controlled.

Sure, it was simpler to live in Grandpa's old house. No insulation, no pollution, no condensation. But then again, you had to warm up one side at a time to the old wood stove and cut a lot of wood.

We are asking the walls of our house to keep out the elements and hold in warm or cool air at the same time that we are asking our heating and cooling systems to function as economically as possible. To accomplish that we need to understand how all of this works. Here are some of the answers.

**Q** I am thinking about buying a house that is heated with a propane heating system. If I do buy the house, will it be possible to change the heating system to oil?

**A** If you were changing from oil to propane, there would not be a problem. The determining factor here is the chimney. Chimneys for propane systems are relatively small, while chimneys for oil systems are much larger. The oil system also requires more space. It is possible that when the house was built the chimney was designed for an oil furnace. If that is the case, there is no problem converting because the chimney will be large enough. If the house you are thinking of buying was built with a chimney for propane, there could be problems changing to oil. There is a possibility that it can be done if you purchase a new oil heating system that is very efficient. If your house does have a smaller propane chimney, have a heating specialist take a look.

**Q** My husband and I are going to buy a new house. We have not yet decided what kind of heating system to buy. What kind of maintenance is required for gas and oil systems?

**A** A gas furnace should be serviced at least once every two years by a professional serviceman. Oil furnaces should receive the same treatment once a year. For the oil system, this includes everything from checking the furnace completely to looking up the chimney. In terms of what maintenance you will have to do yourself, you should check the filters in either oil or gas furnaces at least once a month, and while you are doing that you should make sure that the fan belt in the air-blowing mechanism is not loose. Beyond that, there is not much else that you can (or should) do yourself. If the flame inside the furnace is not a sharp, clean flame, but looks dirty and wild *(see illustration on page 98)*, you should call your serviceman.

**Q** I want to use a wood stove as a primary heat source. Which stove gets the most heat out of a cord of wood?

**A** Like everything in the field of energy conservation, both wood stoves and how we burn wood has evolved a lot in just the last decade. A low-smoldering fire produces a lot of smoke, wastes energy, and can be downright hazardous. Just because a load of wood lasts a long time when smoldered does not mean it is burning efficiently. The smoke in the chimney is like throwing away firewood, and worse, it can lead to a dangerous chimney fire. You can reduce smoke emissions and wasted energy by burning smaller, hotter fires. Split your wood a little smaller and put less in at each loading. Make sure the wood is flaming brightly until it is reduced to charcoal. You will get more heat from your firewood this way, and you will not risk having a chimney fire. A certified low-emission stove (certified to EPA or CSA B415) uses firebox insulation, a large baffle, and super-heated combustion air jets to burn the wood completely before it leaves the firebox. Have the dealer choose one whose size matches the size of your house. You'll find a certified and properly-sized stove much easier and economical to use, and you'll get more heat out of each cord of wood.

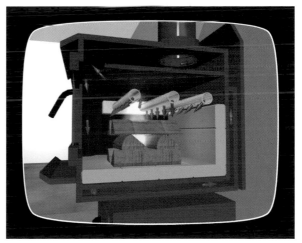

 **For more detail, click on "Heating" on the home screen of the CD-ROM.**

**Q** I like to stay on top of the main-tenance in my house but the furnace rather mystifies me. What can I do myself to help keep it operating optimally?

**A** Most importantly, check the filters regularly and change them when they are clogged enough to slow down the air going through the furnace. Listen to the furnace. If the fan is rattling, tighten up the fan belt. You can even learn a lot about your furnace by taking a close look at the flame. A flame that burns wildly wastes energy and soils the inside of the heat exchanger as well as the chimney. An oil furnace should have a sharp, well-defined flame that doesn't appear to float left and right and has no sign of smoke. A gas flame should not float about and it should not be yellow but more red with a clear, sharp blue center. Have a furnace specialist in to perform a check-up and a tune-up every year for an oil furnace, every two years for a gas furnace.

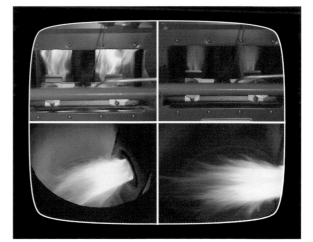

**For more detail, click on "Heating" on the home screen of the CD-ROM.**

**Q** I installed a new furnace in my town house last year. Since then I have noticed that cooking odors and smoke are entering my house. I assume they are coming from my neighbors, since I never use my fireplace and always keep the damper shut. Is it possible the odors are coming from my chimney or furnace?

**A** The problem may lie with your fireplace. It is more than likely that your neighbor's smoke and cooking odors are drifting above the town house and entering your house through the fireplace. Even if you keep the damper closed, there may still be a backdraft that is taking place. This might occur when the exhaust fan is operating or the clothes dryer is on. Cover the front of the fireplace with a plastic seal, making sure that it is airtight, and then see if the problem persists. If it does, you will at least know that the odors are not entering your house through the fireplace. If the fireplace is the problem, you might think about sealing it permanently if you do not use it. The problem may also lie with your furnace chimney. Check for odors in the furnace room while exhaust fans are operating and the furnace is off. If the furnace chimney is backdrafting, you will need a combustion air supply to the furnace room.

**Q** I clean the electronic air filter for my furnace regularly in the dishwasher, but it never seems to work as well as it did when it was new. Do these filters wear out?

**A** Your problem probably lies with your dishwasher and choice of soap. Using the dishwasher to clean electronic air cleaners is not a good idea as the water jets are too strong and the rack can bend the delicate parts of air cleaners. Secondly, most soaps leave a very fine white residue on the plates and wires of air cleaners. This film greatly reduces the effectiveness of the unit. You need cleaners that are good degreasers but, more importantly, rinse off completely, leaving no residue. If you have trouble finding specialized cleaners, concentrate on extensive rinsing with a garden hose and perhaps a little brushing with a soft paintbrush. Let the air cleaner dry thoroughly before turning it on again.

**Q** How can I get rid of the dirty marks around my floor registers without getting carried away with fancy furnace filters?

**A** You can buy filters that are designed to be placed directly under each floor register. This gives you real, localized, room-by-room control. These filters come with a self-adjusting cardboard frame that allows you to simply lift off the register cover, push the filter into the duct and the flaps on the filter will hold it nicely in place. Replace the cover. Remember, they will eventually clog up with all the stuff they catch, so if the heat slows down in that room, remember to change the filter. For those of you who like a very light fragrance in the house, you can get scented versions of this filter. In fact, this is an energy-efficient way to give different rooms of your house different scents or no scents at all, according to your tastes.

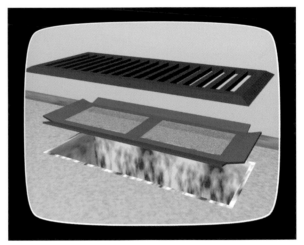

 For more detail, click on "Heating" on the home screen of the CD-ROM.

**Q** My house was built in 1954 with brick exterior walls and plaster interior walls. The house is extremely cold in the winter, particularly near the plaster walls. I have added insulation to the attic in the hope of trapping heat in the house, but it has not done the trick. What else can I do?

**A** The first thing to do is determine what is between the exterior brick wall and the interior plaster wall. There will be either a second brick wall or a hollow stud wall. One way of finding out is to remove the faceplate from the electrical box on the exterior of the house. If you look to the side of the opening, you should be able to see if there is a hollow space or not. If there is a hollow stud wall, you can add fiberglass insulation. If you add the insulation, you will have to hire a contractor who will drill holes in various parts of the wall and add the insulation with a hose. The holes, of course, will have to be filled and the wall repaired. If there is a second brick wall or if you discover the hollow stud wall already has insulation, there is not much you can do from the exterior. What you can do is install rigid foam paneling to the plaster walls inside and install some drywall over that. This will not prevent all the heat loss, but it will certainly help.

**Q** I installed an addition to my house this past summer using rigid foam panels. The end result is that where the old and the new walls meet there is exposed brick on the inside of the house which turned into ice this winter. What is causing it and what can I do to repair it?

**A** As we have seen (above), all brick houses have a small air space between the inside stud wall and the outside brick wall. If you have added a wall perpendicular to the brick wall, that air space goes freely beyond the new wall, letting cold air get to what is now an inside brick wall. You must seal that air flow. Drill holes in the brick wall, between each brick from the top of the wall to the bottom of the wall, along the vertical corner where the new and the old walls meet. Do this on the inside and later cover the walls with trim. Make sure that you drill deep enough to enter the cavity between the brick wall and the stud wall. Through each hole, inject some foam insulation. Once you have gone from bottom to top, there will be a narrow, continuous strip of foam where you separate inside from outside.

**Q** A year ago I built a detached garage next to my house, with a cement floor and 2x6 construction walls. I did a meticulous job with vapor barriers. The problem is that in each corner, about 15 cm (6 in.) above grade, the wall is soaking wet. Outside, the edges are bone dry. What's the problem?

**A** My first reaction is that the problem may lie with a strong, cold wind combined with poor, or no, insulation in the corners, thus causing condensation, or a combination of wind and rain leaking through the garage in the corners. If the damage is occurring from the outside, possibly your flashings are poorly placed and excess water is dripping down on the affected areas. If the problem is inside, it is most likely an insulation problem. Often, when a building is being constructed, the walls and attic are well insulated, but the corners are neglected. My guess is that the moisture in the corners is being caused by condensation from the inside. A quick fix to this problem is to install a piece of rigid foam insulation from ceiling to floor, 5 cm x 5 cm (2 in. x 2 in.), cut at 45°. Do this for all four corners. You will lose a small triangle of space in all four corners, but the added insulation should correct the problem.

**Q** The previous owners of our 80-year-old house had put insulation in the attic. Leaky shingles on the roof and a bathroom vent that shot up directly into the attic has caused the insulation to flatten considerably. We are going to replace the shingles and install a bathroom exhaust. Once that is done, is it necessary to replace the flattened insulation, or is it possible to somehow salvage it?

**A** Whether or not you can salvage the flattened insulation depends on what kind of insulation it is. If it is fiberglass or rock wool, it can be fluffed back to its original appearance. You can use any garden tool or a large-shaped fork to do the trick. If the insulation is cellulose, you will have to replace it. Cellulose insulation becomes hard when wet, turning into something similar to papier-mâché. The flattened insulation may have blocked some of the vents, so be sure that they are clear of any blockage. While you are at it, check for rotten wood. Lastly, it is very important that you redirect the bathroom exhaust out of the attic and not out the soffits, where the hot moist air can simply rise back into the attic.

**Q** I have an old brick house that has been stripped of all walls except the outside brick wall and the open stud wall. I want to seal all air holes from the inside and install insulation in between the stud wall and the brick wall. How should I seal the air holes, and what kind of insulation should I use?

**A** Essentially, you want to do the job backward, starting with the brick wall and working your way in. The problem is that your stud wall is already up and you can't attach anything to the outside of it. First you must understand that it is necessary to have a 2.5 cm (1 in.) air space between the brick and the rest of the wall. This space allows water to drain out of the wall and allows the brick to dry. That is why it is not wise to shoot any of the insulating foams right up against the brick. Make sure there are flashed holes at the bottom of the wall to drain the wall outdoors. Your problem is that the wind will move around in that space. Normally there is a weather barrier, such as building paper, or an air barrier, like house wraps, separating that air space from the sheathing and stud wall. So your challenge is to create a barrier that does not touch the brick, will be waterproof but permeable, and not let the air blow into the fiberglass. Try squeezing in some rigid foam panels between the studs. (Treat the exposed side of the studs with wood preservative before squeezing in the panels.) Then fill the wall with fiberglass and finish with a good vapor barrier.

**Q** What are the advantages and disadvantages of different types of insulation?

**A** Insulation comes in a variety of shapes, sizes, materials, and prices. Use the least expensive kind that does the job, and then pay more for special features like moisture resistance or higher R-value. Fiberglass blankets are commonly found in walls, attics, and floors. They are easy to cut and install, but are susceptible to air leaks. Loose fill fiberglass and cellulose fiber are good insulation for flat ceilings. Unless, however, the homeowner has experienced with these products, they do require professional installation. When installing fiberglass blankets, loose fill fiberglass, and cellulose fiber, protective gear is required. Extruded polystyrene boards are used primarily over walls and foundations. They are resistant to air and vapor penetration and have a higher R-value, but are relatively expensive.

**Q** The insulation in my basement runs only 75 cm (30 in.) down. I plan to finish the basement, which means tearing down the walls. Should I insulate them from top to bottom? If so, should there be an air space between the vapor barrier and the outside block wall?

**A** It is always better to insulate from the ceiling to the floor. Even if the bottom half of the wall is below ground level, there will always be some heat loss without full insulation. The main reason that some newer houses are insulated only halfway is because it is less expensive to build them that way. Install a moisture barrier on the block to grade. Over that, install fiberglass insulation and a vapor barrier. Air spaces can transport moisture to the top and rot the floor. If air spaces are behind the studs, fill them with insulation.

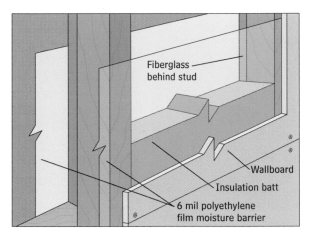

Fiberglass behind stud

Wallboard

Insulation batt

6 mil polyethylene film moisture barrier

**Q** I have a layer of insulation with a vapor barrier in my attic. I want to add another layer of insulation on top of the vapor barrier. Can I do this?

**A** The vapor barrier should always be on the bottom. The way you have it set up now is the worst possible scenario. The vapor barrier is holding moisture in the layer of insulation below and that vapor barrier is exposed to the cold side of the attic. This will result in moisture buildup. You should flip the order so that the vapor barrier is on the floor and the insulation on top. Since you already have the insulation on the bottom, there is one possible solution to your problem. If there is the space in the attic, install double the amount of insulation on top of the vapor barrier. If the barrier remains warm, you should be safe. It would be best, however, to reverse the order of your setup. Keep the vapor barrier on the "warm in winter" side.

**Q** I have a water heating system in my 10-year-old house. Can I heat the garage floor by installing hot-water pipes under a poured concrete surface, and if I can, what is the best way to install the pipes?

**A** The first thing that you should do is lay sheets of rigid foam insulation on the ground. Cover the rigid foam with gravel, and install the pipes in the gravel. Over that, pour the concrete and let it set. This is an excellent way to heat the garage, but there is one hitch: Once you have installed the pipes and covered them with concrete, you are committed to keeping the temperature of those pipes above zero. You must not let them freeze. If they do, the pipes will burst. For safety, you should add bypass, cutoff, and drainage valves.

**Q** I recently bought a very old house. I am concerned that some of the insulation wrapped around the pipes leading from the hot-water tank is made of asbestos. How can I find out, and should I be concerned?

**A** To find out if the insulation is in fact asbestos, you can take a sample of the material to a laboratory. To find one, look up "Laboratories" in the Yellow Pages. However, it should be pointed out that asbestos poses no real danger if it remains undisturbed. Asbestos is only dangerous when it is crumbled and turned into dust. It can then enter your lungs and create severe health problems. If you are going to remove some of it and take it to a lab, make sure that everyone is out of the house, that the basement is very well ventilated, and that you wear full protective gear. A better solution might be to carefully wrap duct tape over the asbestos that is covering the pipes. If the pipes are covered, no dust will escape, and there will be no danger. It is possible that years from now the asbestos will have to be removed, but the tape is a safe interim solution.

**Q** I live in a semi-detached house where the first-floor bathroom is directly above the furnace in the basement. Both the furnace and the bathroom are beside the fire wall joining my house with my neighbor's. The combined effect is that the bathroom becomes unbearably hot. Is there a way to reduce the amount of heat in the bathroom, or is there a way to redirect the heat throughout the house?

**A** Yes. There should be two control systems there now. If not, they can be installed. On the ducts that extend out from the furnace there are handles that control a small damper inside the duct. You can use those to control the amount of hot air that flows to each floor register. The other area where you can control the amount of heat is in the bathroom itself. The vents, either on the floor or on the wall, should also have a duct control that will allow you to reduce the amount of hot air flow. If the duct is rising straight up and the bathroom is directly above, the bathroom is probably receiving too much air that should be spread throughout the house. You could disconnect the current arrangement and reconnect the bathroom duct to a position 90 cm (3 ft) or so away on the side of the main duct. This too would reduce the air flow to the bathroom.

**Q** In the winter, when the heat is on high, the cushioned flooring in my kitchen rises in a small area directly above the hot-air duct underneath the floor. What can I do to eliminate the problem?

**A** It is impossible to eliminate rising heat from an air duct. It is possible, however, to reduce the amount of heat that gets through the floor. There are many joints in a standard duct system. These joints are natural air loss areas. If you can gain access to the duct under the floor, sealing these joints would improve the situation. In addition, install some insulation over the duct and underneath the floor. This will hold the heat in and what heat does rise will be more evenly distributed and not localized in one section. If adding the insulation does not help, you will have to pull up the cushion flooring and glue it back down.

**Q** I have a detached garage that I use as a workshop. I use an electric heater to keep it warm in the winter, but I want to know if running the clothes dryer vent into the garage would provide any excess heat?

**A** This is not a very good idea for several reasons. The greatest problem that you will encounter is excessive moisture. When you put clothes in the dryer, they are wet. In the drying process, the water in the clothes ends up exiting through the vent system. I guarantee that your tools will rust and you will have problems with condensation everywhere inside the garage. The only way that you could provide heat from the dryer without the moisture is to run the dryer without any clothing inside. As you know, running a dryer requires a good amount of electricity and it would not be very economical. To add to that, if your garage is detached from the house, most of the heat will be lost where the vent runs outside between the house and the garage.

**Q** I bought a house about two years ago. Over the last two winters I have found the temperature in the basement to be quite low. A friend commented that the honeycomb surface of the basement concrete wall might be the reason for the cool temperatures. Is my friend's assessment correct, and why does the wall have a honeycomb surface?

**A** The reason that the concrete wall has a honeycomb look to it is because the contractor did not mix the concrete properly. It does not mean that there is any structural flaw in the wall. Honeycombed or not, the concrete wall is worth less than R-1, which means that as much as 20 percent of your heating bill goes through those walls. If there is no water leakage through the wall, there is not much to worry about. Apply some parging to the honeycomb wall. After it dries, I would suggest adding some insulation. The best, and easiest, insulation to add flush to a concrete wall is rigid foam paneling, and over that some drywall. You will lose a little bit of floor space in the basement, but it will be much warmer and your heating bills will drop.

**Q** I am having a problem with condensation on the windows in my living room. I have blinds over the windows and a heat vent on the floor directly under the windows. The vent blows hot air toward the inside of the room. Someone told me the problem is that the heat from the floor vent is not hitting the windows directly. Is this correct?

**A** This is correct. The reason that radiators and floor vents are located directly under windows is because condensation and heat loss are most likely to occur there. If the floor vent is pushing hot air toward the middle of the room, the windows are not exposed to enough heat. Either turn the vent controls so that the air shoots straight up, or if the vent has a deflector tent over it, remove it. The second thing that you can do to provide more heat to the window area is to move the blinds in from the window as much as 15 cm (6 in.). Most people when installing blinds install them flush with the window. Again, any heat rising will bypass the window and rise to the ceiling on the room side of the blinds. Eliminate those two problems and the condensation should stop.

**Q** I have a cantilevered addition to my house that extends out about 60 cm (2 ft). In the winter, those 60 cm (2 ft) of flooring become very cold. Is there any way to heat the affected area without having to rip up the flooring?

**A** There is no easy solution to this problem. Any heat rising from the basement will warm the floors above. With a cantilever floor, there is no heat coming from below, but just cold air. There are some things that can be done to improve the situation. The first thing to do is remove the quarter-round molding where the inside wall and floor meet. Fill that space with caulking. Outdoors, underneath the cantilevered section, caulk all cracks, and add sheets of rigid foam paneling and another layer of plywood over that. If you have forced-air heating, extend the duct to run through the floor area that is affected. If that is too difficult to get to, electric heating coils or electric heating blankets made to install under rugs could do the same job. One last trick that will improve the situation is an old one—lay a rug on the floor.

**Q** I have a new gas-fired boiler heating an old house. It heats water in cast-iron radiators. I bought a setback thermostat that turns on the heat one hour before I get up in the morning. Yet the house is cold when I rise. What is wrong?

**A** Setback thermostats are designed primarily for forced-air furnaces, which recuperate heat very quickly. Cast-iron radiators take a little longer to heat up, about two hours. All you have to do is set the timer to activate the heat one hour earlier. You should also set the timer to turn off the heat one hour earlier than you now do because the

same principle is involved but in reverse. Another trick to help increase the heat coming from the cast-iron radiators is to strip them of their paint. Paint is one of the best insulators and it literally holds the heat back. If you do want them painted, use a thin layer of metallic paint which will radiate the heat.

# VENTILATION

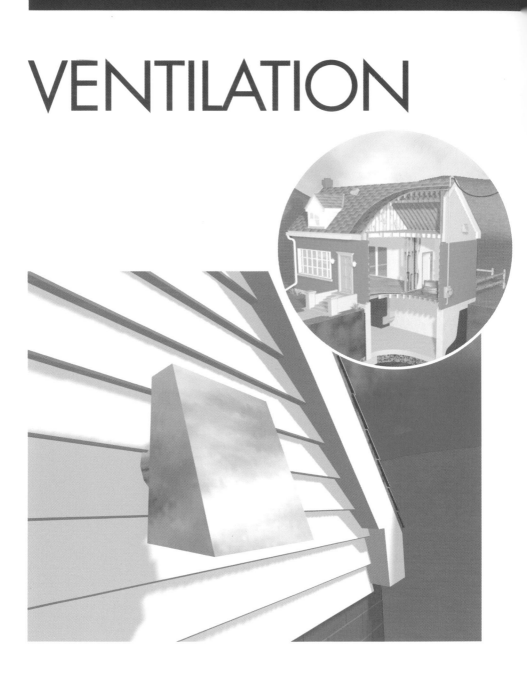

# CHAPTER 6

Making the move from the drafty old houses of our grandparents to our own modern, well-insulated homes has forced us to learn a lot about what the wind used to do for us. It used to blow in one side of the house, pick up moisture and other pollutants, and blow them out the other side of the house. All those cold air drafts made sure that every room in the house had fresh air, and the house was so dry that we rarely had any condensation problems. What we didn't see is that with little or no insulation in the walls, the heat kept the walls and attic dry as well, so our grandparents' houses lasted a long time.

Today we don't want cold air drafts and demand inexpensive heating. Insulating our homes has necessitated air barriers and vapor barriers to protect the walls and attic from frost and rot. Now it is up to us to do the job the wind used to do. We need ventilation to get rid of pollutants, especially from the kitchen and bathroom. We need to bring fresh air into the house rather than rely on cold air drafts. We need to be sure that the air is filtered, perhaps even cleaned and distributed to every room of the house. The chapter that follows addresses the answers to some of these questions that were once written on the wind.

**Q** I often feel unwell in my own home, but never when I am next door, house-sitting at my neighbor's. I have read about "sick building syndrome"; can a house be affected as well?

**A** Mountain air is great, but we prefer to live in houses, and the air might not be so healthy in your house. These boxes that we live in protect us from the elements and assure us our privacy, but as we get better and better at boxing out the elements, we also box *in* lots of other things, like air pollutants. There are two categories of pollutants floating around in the air in your house: biological contaminants such as dust mites and mold, and chemical contaminants such as solvents coming out of building materials and furnishings. These are likely the cause of your symptoms. There are three steps to getting these things under control and maintaining a healthy atmosphere in your house. First, eliminate whatever sources of pollution you can by simply getting them out of your house: throw out moldy rugs and books; store solvents and cleaners outside; replace furniture, carpets, and underlay that give off odors and organic compounds with cleaner substitutes. (Rubber-based underlay in particular is a major offender.) Second, separate or isolate things you cannot eliminate. That might mean a coat of varnish on the underside of particleboard countertops. Then ventilate to lower concentrations of what is left by replacing polluted air with fresh air. With a little thought about the house we live in, we can greatly improve the quality of the air we breathe.

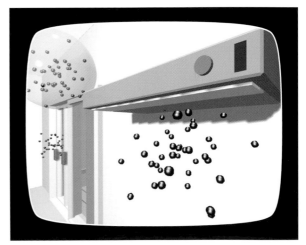

 For more detail, click on "Interiors" on the home screen of the CD-ROM.

**Q** I have a problem with excessive dust in my house, and I want to install an electronic air filter to tackle the problem. Which electronic air filter is considered the best and should it be installed to the supply air duct or to the return air duct?

**A** Whether they are installed in your heater or in your air conditioner, electronic air filters will always filter dust in the return air duct. By filtering the air before it enters the appliance, an electronic air filter serves two functions. First, it protects the inside of the air conditioner or heater from dust. Second, it ensures that the treated air leaving the air conditioner or heater is clean. Electronic air filters are excellent and work very well provided they are monitored and cleaned regularly. If they are cleaned regularly, they will work at about 95 percent efficiency. If they are not cleaned regularly, their air-cleaning capacity is reduced rapidly. HEPA filters are the best nonelectronic disposable filters. They are expensive, but good enough to use in hospitals. Electrostatic filters are also good. Last, there are ordinary pleated filters and the standard furnace filter that protects the furnace but does not clean the air.

**Q** I have noticed some discoloration on the north wall in my house. The discoloration comes in streaks running vertically from the floor to the ceiling. What can I do to remove them?

**A** As you know, the north wall in any house is going to be the coldest. The streaks that you have on the wall are nothing more than dirt stains. The reason that they are there is because a drop in temperature will create more moisture on the wall, and allow more dirt and dust to cling to it. The dirt is showing up in streaks because they are following the 2x4 studs lying behind the drywall. The insulation between the drywall and the outside wall is placed in between the studs. The studs themselves are not insulated, and the wall in front of the studs are colder than the rest of the wall. What you have to do is insulate the studs. The easiest way to do that is to install rigid foam paneling over the studs. You can either tear down the existing drywall, install the paneling, and erect new drywall, or place a 2.5 cm (1 in.) sheet of rigid foam over the existing drywall and add a new drywall over that. This is the simplest way to correct the problem, however, you will have to make the electrical boxes and window frames flush with the new wall.

**Q** I have mold in my windows and in the corners of some of the rooms of my house. How dangerous is this stuff?

**A** Mold forms wherever there is chronic moisture, like summertime condensation in the basement or wintertime condensation on windows and the northeast and northwest corners of some rooms. Mold is constantly sending out spores as it reproduces. These spores are what can aggravate or even cause asthma in some people. The problem is that these spores, invisible to the naked eye, float very lightly and can take hours to reach the floor—and are constantly stirred up every time you walk across the room. You must not let mold live in your house. You must kill it and wash away the dead material. Use a one-to-one mixture of standard laundry bleach and water with a little dishwasher soap. The bleach will kill the mold and the soap will clean off the wall. If it is heavy, wear a protective mask to not breathe a concentration of spores. If you have moldy furniture or books that are difficult to clean, throw them away. Just airing them out will not eliminate spores that will lie dormant waiting for a bit of moisture to grow again.

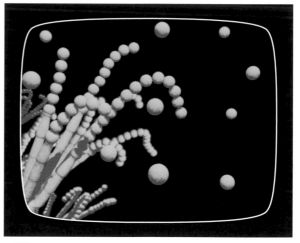

 For more detail, click on "Interiors" on the home screen of the **CD-ROM**.

**Q** I plan to remove a wall in my living room. I am concerned about my ventilation system because there is a vent on either side of the wall I plan to take down. What should I be concerned about, and how should I tackle the situation?

**A** I think you should be concerned about what kind of wall you are planning to remove. If it is a support wall, do not remove it or the ceiling will collapse. A support wall will run perpendicular to the direction of the joists underneath the floor. A wall running parallel with the joists is not likely to be a support wall. If you have any doubts about whether it is a support wall or not, have a building inspector take a look at it. Once you have determined that it is safe to remove the wall, and you have done so, vents can be installed on the floor itself. They do not have to be on the wall at a 90° angle. The only problem you may encounter is if you plan to place a piece of furniture over the new vent site. If this is the case, and the vent's location on the floor surface is going to be a problem, then you will have to find another area in the same room to install a vent, and of course, that will require restructuring the system behind the walls and in the basement. This is something that I suggest you avoid because it is a costly, time-consuming, and laborious affair. If the new location of the vent is not a problem, there are a great number of vents available today, and not just the standard metal grate type. There are wood vents that will match the color and wood type of the floor itself, so they will blend in and not be noticeable.

**Q** I installed an electric furnace at the cottage and added a heat pump to provide air conditioning. I want to install the same system in my house, but have been advised to install a gas furnace with an air conditioner instead. What should I do?

**A** The question of which one to use depends on where you live and the climate. Using electricity is the most expensive method to heat a house, except in Quebec, where electrical rates are the lowest in North America. If you live in an area where gas is readily available, and therefore inexpensive, using it and a separate air conditioner would be less expensive than the complete electric heat pump system. If however, you live in an area where gas is expensive, or perhaps not available at all, and you have to heat the house with electricity, the complete heat pump system will be better.

**Q** I need to improve the air quality in my house. Why are there so many different ventilation systems to choose from?

**A** All ventilation systems are designed to prevent the buildup of indoor air pollutants and make your house a healthier place to live, but they can vary from simple exhaust fans to high-tech, whole-house air systems. Your choice depends on your air quality and whether you are looking for a minimum or maximum solution. The range-hood exhaust fan is a prime example of a simple solution. It removes a lot of air for short periods of time on demand. It is used together with a whole-house system for areas like kitchens, bathrooms, and workshops. Adding a fresh-air duct to the return air plenum of the furnace is better than relying on cold-air drafts to replace the air the exhaust fans throw outdoors. An air-change ventilator does the same thing more efficiently. Usually a single box with two fans, it moves air both into and out of the house. A heat recovery ventilator (HRV) does the same job but also traps most of the heat from the exhaust air and uses it to warm up the fresh air coming in, saving significantly on heating costs. A new breed of ventilation system, the energy recovery ventilator (ERV), also uses exhaust heat to preheat the fresh air but brings back some of the moisture to maintain a good humidity balance in houses that become too dry with continuous ventilation, recuperating even more heat and eliminating static electricity.

**For more detail, click on "Ventilation" on the home screen of the CD-ROM.**

Ventilator

**Q** **There are con-
densation spots**
on the ceiling of the
addition to my house.
The addition is ventilat-
ed with a turbine roof
ventilator that sits atop
the roof. I suspect that
the condensation is
coming from the attic
above. What can I do to
correct the problem?

**A** If water is leaking from above, it is usually
caught by the vapor barrier in the attic.
Condensation on the ceiling is usually a sign of a
very cold spot that collects moisture from house
air. Turbines, installed too close to loose fill insulation, can lift the insulation out of the attic and
blow it away. Turbines do draw air out of the attic,
but how much they draw is completely uncontrol-
lable. If there is no wind on a hot summer day,
when some attic ventilation might be welcome,
they are no better than a passive vent. When the
wind blows hard, the turbines kick in, sometimes
drawing warm, moist air from the house into the
cold attic. They are often noisy and have a tendency of freezing and drawing snow into the attic.
Check the ceiling, making sure that the condensation spots are well covered with insulation, and
replace your turbine with a passive vent. These
stand high above the roof, preventing snow from
entering the attic, and come with round bases to
replace turbines without having to modify the roof
flashing.

**Q** I want to install an exhaust fan in my bathroom. Can I buy a fan that will attach to the wall and not the ceiling? If so, are they made to turn on automatically?

**A** Yes is the answer to both questions. Wall fans are better than ceiling fans because the heat and moisture that is being pulled through the fan often causes problems in a cold attic. Ideally, a fan should run down and out the basement instead of up and out the roof. If you buy a humidistat switch and attach it to the manual switch, it will turn on and off automatically. The switch can be set to accept the desired amount of humidity in the room. When the humidity level in the bathroom rises above that set level, the fan will activate automatically. There are even some fans that activate with motion detectors.

**Q** The bathroom in my house has neither a window nor an exhaust fan. As a result, a considerable amount of mildew has formed where the wall and ceiling meet. What can I do to get rid of the mildew?

**A** This is a condensation problem, and there are several possible solutions. The first thing to do is simply eliminate the mildew. Mildew is a toxic organism that can be very dangerous to all who use the bathroom. Clean it with a one-to-one solution of water and regular laundry bleach. Be sure to wear gloves and goggles to protect yourself. After you have cleaned the wall and ceiling, and allowed them to dry properly, apply a paint that specifically contains fungicides. This will protect the surface against future mildew better than a regular paint. The mildew has formed because the bathroom is not properly ventilated. Next, an exhaust fan is absolutely essential. If the bathroom does not have a window, there is no other possible way to allow the moisture to escape. Check the insulation in the attic just above this area. Little or no insulation will cause the condensation and mildew to return. If you cannot get to the attic, add rigid foam insulation on the bathroom ceiling.

**Q** I want to finish a room in my attic, but the bathroom fan from below obstructs the floor. Do I need a new fan?

**A** You need a fan that has duct connections on both the input and the output, allowing it to be placed absolutely anywhere along the duct run. These are called in-line fans. You install a round grill on the ceiling of the bathroom, connect the ducting to that, run the ducting around your attic renovation, connecting to the motor in the small roof section above the new attic, and then out. My preference is to avoid all that cold attic area and put the exhaust grill on an inside wall of the bathroom, run the duct into the basement, install the motor someplace convenient in the basement and run the exhaust out the bottom of the house. Not only will these in-line fans go anywhere, but they are powerful enough for long runs and you can put multiple outlets on the same run, such as venting the basement bathroom at the same time. Some models have an ingenious backward inclined airfoil blade that makes them whisper quiet and dust-free.

 For more detail, click on "Ventilation" on the home screen of the CD-ROM.

**Q** An exhaust fan was installed in the bathroom last year. I heard that they should be periodically checked for efficiency. Is this true, and if so, how do I check it?

**A** Yes, they should be checked every year. There are two reasons for this. An exhaust fan is designed to draw moisture from the bathroom and send it outside. Along with the moisture, the fan is going to draw dirt and dust. Not all of that dirt and dust is going to exit the house. Some may remain in the exhaust and slightly impede the action of the fan. The second reason that the fan should be checked is that if it is not working properly, the higher levels of humidity in the bathroom will cause damage. There is a very simple way to check the system. A large garbage bag, a coat hanger, and some duct tape are all the materials required. Bend the frame of the coat hanger into a square. Then tape the opening edge of the garbage bag to the coat hanger. Turn on the exhaust fan and place the garbage bag over the exhaust end of the fan outside. The garbage bag should fill with air within three or four seconds. If it takes longer, the system should be cleaned. You can do the same thing with the exhaust inside, but make sure that the garbage bag is inflated. If it takes longer than three or four seconds for the bag to deflate, the ducts should be inspected and the fan cleaned.

**Q** Is it true that a whole-house fan can effectively circulate air in a house?

**A** A whole-house fan can do an effective job of circulating house air in areas that have cool, dry nights. They are not quite as effective as air conditioners, but they do a good job. Whole-house fans are cheaper than air conditioners, and use much less electricity. The fan, usually located in the attic over a central hallway, is designed to draw hot house air into the attic, where it escapes through attic vents. At least one door or window has to be left open when the fan is operating to pull the air through the house. Many fans come equipped with timers, speed controls, and thermostats. During the winter, the fan opening must be covered with an insulated panel and sealed airtight to prevent moist, warm air from escaping into the attic. For this reason, whole-house fans are rarely used outside of the southern United States.

**Q** I have an exhaust fan in my second-floor bathroom. The system runs through the ceiling and then turns at a 90° angle and exits through the outside wall. There has been a condensation buildup where the exhaust pipe runs parallel with the ceiling. How can I correct the problem?

**A** There are two possible reasons for the condensation buildup. First, the damper on the outside exhaust hood is either stuck open or missing. This allows freezing cold air into the duct, which chills the ceiling below. The second possibility is that cold air is coming into the ceiling area through the opening in the outside wall between the exhaust duct and the wall. You should seal this with foam in a can, not just fiberglass. On a brick veneer wall, the exhaust duct must be watertight to the brick and airtight to the sheathing behind the brick. Also ensure that it slopes to the outside to drain any condensation outdoors.

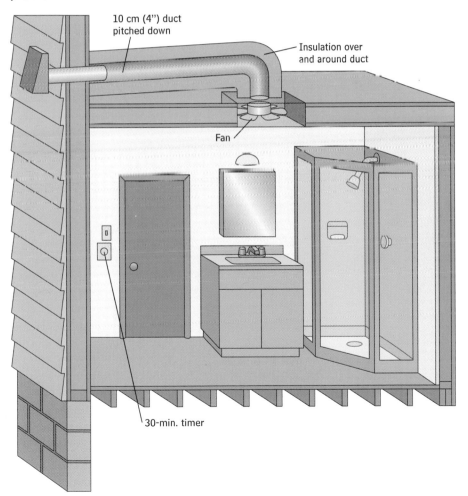

10 cm (4") duct
pitched down

Insulation over
and around duct

Fan

30-min. timer

**Q** A bedroom above my garage becomes extremely cold during the winter. Is there anything that can be done to improve the overall temperature, and can the cold-air drafts be eliminated?

**A** The fact of the matter is that it is impossible to make a room above a cold storage space equal in temperature to any other room in the house. However, there are ways to improve the situation, and that includes eliminating air drafts. The problem with older houses is that they are rarely sealed properly. The first thing to do is remove the quarter-round molding on the bedroom floor, and caulk the joint shut. If there are any other areas in the room that are likely to be the source of air drafts, caulk them too. Then caulk the joint where the garage wall and the floor above meet. These joints are rarely done properly, if at all. Immediately there will be a noticeable difference. Then I would suggest installing some fiberglass insulation on the garage ceiling and placing a drywall ceiling over that. Improving the insulation and eliminating the air drafts will not make the temperature in the room equal with other rooms in the house, but there will be an improvement.

**Q** There is a cold-air draft that comes through the front door of my house on cold winter days. The previous owners installed weather stripping but it does not seem to be doing the job. What can I do?

**A** In extremely cold climates, it is often necessary to change weather stripping every year. People seem to think that once stripping is installed, it will work well for years to come. This is not the case. However, even if the weather stripping for the door is new, and in good shape, the cold weather may warp the door slightly, in which case the existing stripping needs to be adjusted. The cold air that is coming through the door may be only in one specific part of the door. There are two ways to find out. Close the door on a piece of paper. If you can pull the paper out there is little or no protection in that area. If the paper is stuck and you cannot pull it out, the stripping is doing the job. Try moving the paper along the edges of the door until you find the warped area. Or you can open a window on the other side of the house and hold a cigarette or incense up to the door. The forced draft will indicate where the problem is by drawing the smoke through the door. Loosen the screws to adjust the weather stripping and repeat either method until the draft is eliminated.

**Q** I live in a two-story house that sits on concrete and does not have a basement. The living room is difficult to keep warm in the winter. All the hot-air vents are located on the ceiling. If I moved them down to the ground, would the room be better heated?

**A** There will always be a problem with heating a room whose hot- and cold-air vents are located on the ceiling. The hot air will descend from the vent and almost immediately rise again. As a result, cold air will sit at the bottom of the room. What you have to do is install a cold-air return vent on the floor. It can be anywhere in the room as long as it is as far away from the hot-air vents as possible, and one vent will be enough to solve the problem. The cold-air return will act as a vacuum and suck all the cold air from the room and send it to the furnace. The cold air will disappear from the room and as a result will pull some of the hot air downward.

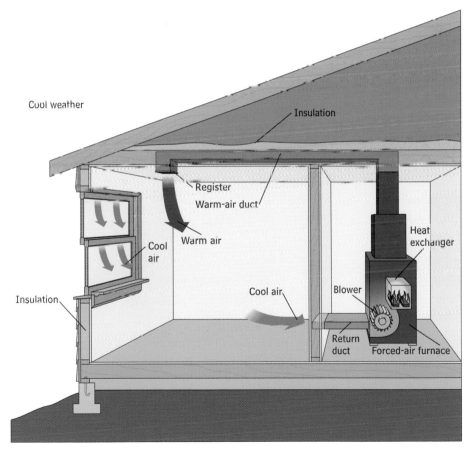

Cool weather

Insulation

Register
Warm-air duct

Warm air

Cool air

Heat exchanger

Cool air

Blower

Insulation

Return duct    Forced-air furnace

# WINDOWS & DOORS

# CHAPTER 7

Windows and doors are more than just holes in our walls. They are like border checkpoints between our homes and the outside world. Doors allow us access, letting us go in and out, while windows give us light, a nice view, and—if they are installed properly—air circulation. Some doors, like patio doors, even act like windows, doing two jobs at once.

Yet most of our troubles with windows and doors arise precisely because they *are* holes in the walls. And whenever you make a hole in a nice, thick, energy-efficient wall, you open a Pandora's box of possibilities: rain to leak in, cold to come through, mold to gather, or any number of complications that you didn't have before you cut the hole in the wall. Going back to our border-crossing analogy, we expect our windows and doors to let in the good elements and keep out the unwanted ones.

So most of the problems we encounter with our windows and doors have to do with what they inadvertently let in: rain in summertime and cold in winter. In fact, far from being a hole in the wall, windows and doors are fairly complicated assemblies. This chapter reveals just how complicated they can be.

**Q** The windows at my cottage are double-paned. I have discovered condensation in between the two panes. What can I do to correct the problem?

**A** Technically, there is no effective way of eliminating the problem. The best way to correct the problem is to replace the glass units. Obviously, seals have broken if there is condensation between the panes. If you can, drill three small 3 mm ($1/8$ in.) diameter holes up through the bottom of the window frame. Make sure that the holes are between the two panes of glass where the condensation has collected. Then drill another hole perpendicular to the first hole. This horizontal hole should connect with the vertical hole and lead outside—not inside. Fill the bottom of the vertical hole with putty. As the sun warms the window during the day, it will drive some of the moisture out through the holes. At night, the holes will draw in dry air. It is a tricky job, but if you are successful, it will clear up the windows without affecting their energy efficiency.

**Q** I have a single-pane window with a metal frame in my basement. The window is fine, but the metal frame is always sweating. What is causing this, and what can I do to eliminate it?

**A** The reason that the frame is sweating is because the window is only a single-pane one and the metal does not have a thermal break between the inside and the outside. The metal brings in the cold temperatures and moist indoor air condenses on the metal surface. The only solution to this problem is adding a second window. If you want to do a temporary job, you can simply cover the window with some plastic sheeting, but the plastic should be at least 12 mm ($1/2$ in.) in front of the metal, or it too will get cold. Ideally you should add a second window, or change the whole thing for a modern energy-efficient window.

**Q** We have a sliding glass door that faces onto our back deck. Every time it rains, water seeps inside at the bottom of the sliding door. The deck outside is sloped away from the house, so I know that the problem is not water buildup on the deck. I am at a loss as to what may be causing the leak. What can I do to find out?

**A** There are several things that you should look at to determine where the water is entering through the sliding door. The first thing to do is make sure that the frame is properly caulked to the house. If not, redo the caulking. The next thing that you should look at is the base of the frame where the door sits and slides. There should be several drainage holes in the frame that extend outside. If they are not there, they should be. If they are there, they may be blocked and water that would normally drain properly has nowhere to escape. If the problem lies elsewhere, then I presume that it is the weather stripping or the door frame itself. One way to isolate the problem is to have someone spray water on the outside of the door in specific spots while someone else on the inside of the door places some folded toilet paper along the bottom of the frame. As soon as the water enters, the toilet paper will change color and indicate where the water is leaking in.

**Q** I am building a new house. What is the best way to protect the tops of the outside window frames from water damage?

**A** The best way to protect the window frame from water damage is to install a drip cap flashing. This Z-shaped piece of metal fits under the shingles or siding, above the window frame. The other side of the drip cap flashing hangs over the window frame, allowing water to drip over the frame and not onto it. Even if water gets underneath the shingles or siding, the drip cap flashing will divert the water out of harm's way. Keep the flashing sloped to drain off the water.

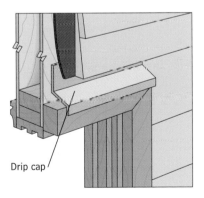

Drip cap

127

**Q** I am the second owner of an eight-year-old house. All the windows in the house are wooden casement windows that crank open. When it rains, water enters the house between the glass and the window frame. Why are windows that are only eight years old reacting to the elements this way, and what can I do to correct the problem?

**A** There is no simple answer to why there is damage to your window frames after only eight years. It is possible that the windows were not properly installed, weather conditions adversely affected them, or the windows themselves are not of high quality. There are two possible solutions to your problem. The longer and more laborious method is to first remove the existing molding where the glass and the frame meet and then remove the glass pane itself. After carefully cleaning the bottom of the wooden frame, apply a bed of silicone caulking. This will prevent any further damage to the window frame. The second possible solution is to remove just the molding from the outside of the window, clean it thoroughly and, after allowing it to dry completely, reseal it with silicone caulking. This works much better than simply caulking over the wood.

**Q** In order to eliminate a draft, I caulked the edges of my bedroom window. Unfortunately, I caulked the window shut. Now I am unable to open my window. Is there a product that can remove the caulking?

**A** If draft-stop caulking was applied, then there is a simple solution. If silicone or thermal plastic caulking was used, then you will have a little work to do. Draft-stop caulking is designed to be put on in late autumn when keeping cold air out and warm air in becomes important. It can easily be removed the next spring. Simply peel it off as if it was masking tape. Silicone caulking can be removed with a special silicone caulking stripper. Thermal plastic caulking will have to be removed with a knife and elbow grease. This, of course, is a tough job. Another option is to keep the windows caulked shut and install a ventilation system above the window and through the wall. If the caulking was applied to stop any winter drafts, maybe it should stay. With a ventilation system installed, you could then control the amount of air movement in the summer and not worry about any drafts coming through the window in the winter.

**Q** Rain is coming into my house through a closed window. Personnel at the hardware store suggested using either polyurethane caulking, silicone caulking, or latex caulking. I'm confused. Which one is best?

**A** The simple answer is that polyurethane caulking is the best. Oil-based caulking sticks well but tends to crack over time. Pure latex caulking is almost useless. Latex acrylic and thermal plastic caulking are very good, but they too will crack over time, because they have a tendency to shrink and become brittle. Unlike the others, silicone caulking does not crack or shrink and remains very elastic over a prolonged period. Unfortunately, it tends to lose its grip on brick. Polyurethane caulking is the best overall caulking for all outdoor uses. Over 90 percent of it is composed of solids, so it remains very elastic and will not crack. You can also paint over it. It may be a little bit more expensive, but it is a good investment. It will remain in place and do its intended job years longer than the other types.

**Q** Last winter my heating bills were considerably high. I noticed that there was a draft coming from my living room window. I do not want to permanently seal the window, but is there anything that can cut down the draft and be removed in the spring?

**A** There certainly is something that you can do. There are caulkings on the market that are designed to provide an excellent seal and can literally be peeled off at any time. The good thing about this caulking is that when it peels off, paint on the frame will not come off with it. Another possibility is to buy plastic sheeting designed to cover windows in the winter. They are transparent and

come with double-sided tape that you apply to the window's edge. The transparent plastic should then be placed over the window and attached to the tape. Traditionally, plastic sheeting was problematic as it was wrinkled and difficult to see through. Newer types of plastic sheeting, however, are completely clear and shrink under heat. Once the sheeting is properly in place, blow hot air on it from a hair dryer. With patience, you can eliminate the wrinkles completely. Either method will eliminate the air draft and bring down your heating bills considerably.

**Q** I am concerned that my venetian blinds may contain lead. How can I be sure that the blinds do not contain lead?

**A** The blinds that you are referring to are cheaply made plastic blinds that contain lead as a stabilizing agent. After the blinds have been in the sun for a long time, the lead in the blinds breaks down and turns into dust. If the dust is touched, it can make its way into the body. Children and pregnant women are particularly vulnerable. Lead can cause brain damage and other serious problems, so it is very important to make sure that you do not own blinds that contain lead. There are government publications that provide informative instruction on what types of blinds (and other household items) are dangerous. If you are worried that your blinds contain lead, you can buy a product called a lead tester. It is a 7.5 cm (3 in.) tube with a short, bristled end. Squeeze the tube, which secretes a yellow liquid, onto the surface of the blind. After mixing it over the surface with the bristled end, watch to see if the color of the surface turns red. If it does, then the blind contains lead. If it does not turn red, then the blind is lead-free. The gadget is easy to use and not very expensive.

**Q** My living room window is fogging up during the cold winter months. Are the blinds hanging in front of the window in any way responsible?

**A** It is possible that the blinds are a factor for the buildup of condensation of the window. The reason that heaters are located directly in front of windows is because the windows are the parts of the house that are going to let in the most cold air and allow heat to escape. If your blinds are positioned too close to the window, the heat rising from the heater is going to pass the window and rise to the ceiling. Ideally, blinds should be positioned 7.5 to 15 cm (3 to 6 in.) in front of the window. They will still block sunshine, but rising heat will be able to get behind the blinds and heat the window, thus eliminating the condensation. Some blinds come equipped with brackets that extend them out from the window. If your blinds did not come with brackets, extension brackets can be bought at specialty home decorating stores.

**Q** My front door warps and gives me a lot of trouble. In the summer it rattles in the wind and in the winter I can hardly push it hard enough to get the latch to catch and hold it shut. What can I do to stop the warping?

**A** You may help control the warping a bit by painting the top and the bottom edges of the door. Most people never notice these surfaces, but in some doors a lot of moisture gets in and out through these surfaces, aggravating the warping. Other doors are just going to warp, so to maintain a good fit you need to adjust the catch on the door frame from season to season. I have fallen in love with a little piece of hardware that very efficiently solves this problem. It is a striker plate that has a stair-stepped inner piece that fits inside the hole in the door frame. As the tongue from the door latch goes into the striker plate, it ratchets up on the stair step. This means that the door stays tight if the tongue is on the first step, or on the last, but it is no longer banging back and forth inside the hole. You never need to adjust the striker plate, it does it for you all year long.

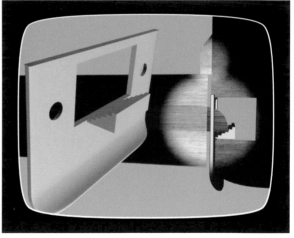

 For more detail, click on "Windows & Doors" on the home screen of the CD-ROM.

**Q** I installed weather stripping on the door frame in the entrance of my house three weeks ago. The stripping on the top and the side where the door swings open are fine, but the stripping on the hinge side of the door has fallen off. Did I not install it properly?

**A** When weather stripping is installed, most people attach it to the door frame. The stripping on the top and the open side will last a year—the standard life expectancy for stripping. The stripping on the hinge side of the frame will be caught in a wiping motion every time the door is closed, and will last only a few weeks. The proper method for installing stripping is to attach it to the frame on the top and open side, but on the hinge side it should be attached to the door itself, not the frame. This way it presses into the frame when the door closes, rather than being side swiped.

**Q** Do I need a locksmith to install a deadbolt lock or is it something that I can do myself?

**A** Yes, you can install a deadbolt lock by yourself. First make an outline of the strike plate on the door jamb using a utility knife. After chiseling a mortise in the door jamb, attach the strike plate with long screws. Most lock kits come with a template designed to facilitate the job for the nonprofessional. Tape the template to the door opposite the strike plate, making sure that they line up together perfectly. Once the template is in place, drill small holes on the dots that will eventually screw the lock into place. In the center of the template, drill a cylinder hole using a hole saw, and install the lock cylinder and backplate in the hole. The lock can now be slipped on and locked into place. Be sure to test the lock's ability to engage and disengage before mounting the final screws.

# PAINTING & STAINING

# CHAPTER 8

Painting and staining are each entire professions unto themselves, and the intense competition from all the paint, stain, and finishing manufacturers doesn't make it any simpler. The problem is that they keep redefining what is a stain and what is a paint, inventing wonderful new products and changing the publicity on the old paints and stains that we thought we had figured out.

Not all of this innovation is market-driven. For example, lead is what once gave old paint its durability and bright colors. Lead has been outlawed in paint for years. Now several states in the United States have followed California's example and have put tight restrictions on solvent-based paints and stains, such as oil paint. That has forced manufacturers to find quality paints, stains, and finishes that are water-based.

Of course, this doesn't help at all when trying to decipher all the information on these wonderful new products, which tells you how fantastic they are, but not whether they are the best choices for your painting projects. So I get lots of questions on painting and staining, and I keep learning more every time I talk to another lab technician or painting professional. Read on to learn more yourself.

**Q** Other than the great difference in price, what are the differences between acrylic and latex paints?

**A** The basic difference between the two paints is that latex paint is water-based and acrylic paint has a chemical composition that gives it elasticity. (Just to confuse us all, there are "acrylic latex" paints, with varying degrees and properties of both.) Outside house paints are moving away from latex to 100 percent acrylic because the latter easily expands and contracts with heat and cold. As a result it holds better than latex. You are right—there is a difference in price. Latex paint is much less expensive, but remember that if you use latex over the more expensive acrylic, the surface will have to be painted again much sooner.

**Q** I want to apply a paint that will brighten my son's bedroom. Since my son has a mild asthma condition I want to know if there is a paint that is safe and if there is a method of painting that will reduce the danger?

**A** You definitely want to use a latex paint. There may be a strong odor, but latex paint is nontoxic. There are some individuals who are sensitive to latex paint, but few are. A high-gloss latex paint will help illuminate the room even more. Obviously, white paint will reflect the most light, but other light colors can also work well. In terms of protecting your son from the odor of the paint, you can place a fan on the window sill that blows air outside while, and after, you paint. Another thing that you can do before you start painting is to install some inexpensive weather stripping on the bedroom door. This will help prevent most of the fumes from exiting the room and entering the rest of the house.

**Q** I dislike using oil paints because of the great difficulties using them. However, I live in a very old house where all the walls are covered with oil paint, and I want to cover them with latex-based paint. I have heard conflicting reports about how to best prepare the walls before covering them with latex. What should I do?

**A** It is simple enough to apply any type of paint over latex, but to apply latex over an oil-based paint is a little tricky. A wall covered with oil-based paint is usually very smooth. Latex paint will have trouble clinging to—or attaching to—a smooth surface. Even if one succeeds in covering oil paint with latex, the two types of paint expand and contract at different rates, and in a short period of time the paint might chip and peel. The solution is to clean the walls with trisodium phosphate (TSP). TSP is fairly caustic, so remember to wear gloves and goggles. Then apply a super-adherent primer specifically formulated to prime oil paint for latex. There are also super-adherent primers that permit painting over ceramic tiles and plastic laminates. This special primer provides the transition between oil paint and new latex.

**Q** I am renovating my bathroom this summer, and I would like to install tongue-and-groove pine wood over drywall. I want to know what is the best way to waterproof the pine?

**A** You can put any kind of finish on the wood. The problem with tongue-and-groove pine is that moisture will always seep through and enter the drywall behind. The first thing to do is cover the drywall with either an oil-based paint or a vapor barrier primer. If any moisture seeps through the pine, it will not be able to penetrate the drywall. However, if the moisture seeping through the pine is stopped at the waterproof drywall, it will penetrate the back side of the pine. To prevent that from happening, cover the side of the pine that will face the drywall with a water sealer. The easiest way to do this is to cover all sides with the sealer at the same time before installing the pieces. Once the waterproofing is completed, any finish can be applied on the exposed pine.

**Q** Can I paint directly over existing wallpaper or must it first be removed? If I have to remove it, what is the easiest and least expensive way to do so?

**A** Yes, you can paint directly over existing wallpaper. However, there are a couple of concerns. The wallpaper seams will be more noticeable after applying the paint because the wallpaper pattern normally hides them. The only possible way to hide them is if you sponge-paint. Whether or not you use the sponge or the roller, it is important to apply a coat of primer so that the final coat will not soak into the wallpaper. If you want the perfectly flat wall, you will have to remove the wallpaper before painting. If the wallpaper was applied in the last few years, it may be dry strippable wallpaper. To find out, simply peel the wallpaper from a corner. If it peels with ease, then continue. If it does not, then you have the old-style wallpaper and a little bit of work will be required to remove the wallpaper completely. Rent an industrial steamer that will soften the existing wallpaper or use wallpaper stripping chemicals that work like paint strippers. Apply a primer/sealer, as you would have if you had not removed the wallpaper, and then a final coat of paint.

**Q** I have some wooden book-shelves on which I applied furniture oil. I want to paint the bookshelves, but I do not know whether I should use an acrylic primer and then an acrylic paint, or an oil-based paint. Which is better?

**A** What kind of paint you choose to apply to your bookshelves is unimportant. Any kind will do the job. What is important is how you prime the bookshelves. The first thing that you should do is gently wipe the surface with mineral spirits. This will remove any oil that is on the surface and will allow future paint to adhere to the surface. Acrylic or oil, you must use a primer/sealer first. This seals the wood and provides adhesion. The finish coat will not soak into the wood, but will stick well to the primer. As a result, fewer coats are necessary. Acrylic paint is fine as a final coat, but oil paint results in a harder surface.

**Q** My cottage has pressed hardboard exterior walls that are beginning to flake, particularly on the edges. With the exception of the original finish that was applied when the cottage was built, the wood has never been treated or painted. I would like to paint the walls, but I want to make sure that no further damage occurs to the wood. How should I paint the walls?

**A** If the hardboard is flaking, you have a problem with water seepage. It is imperative that you seal the hardboard thoroughly to prevent any water from entering. Wash the wall thoroughly with trisodium phosphate (TSP) or bleach. Many people use dishwasher soap to clean walls before painting. This is a big mistake because there are skin softeners added to dish-washing soap to help keep the dishwashers' hands soft. That same moisturizer will prevent paint from attaching itself to the wall. After cleaning the surface, apply two or three coats of sealer, paying special attention to the edges which are more vulnerable to water damage. Apply a coat of primer paint, and then either an exterior latex or an exterior acrylic paint will finish the job. Remember that hardboard is a pressed paper product that will not last forever. You will eventually have to change the siding.

---

**Q** I have had water leakage where the wall and the sliding door meet in my basement suite. My landlord sealed it with some caulking, stopping the leakage. But now some brown stains have appeared on the wall. What are they and what should I do to eliminate them?

**A** First determine if it is mold or a dirt mark. Put a drop of laundry bleach on it. If it is mold, it will turn grey. If it is dirt, it will lighten slightly. After the mold has been killed with bleach, proceed as if it was dirt. The first thing to do is clean the brown stains with trisodium phosphate (TSP). Even though the wall has been cleaned on the surface, the stain may linger underneath. For that reason, use a stain-block paint instead of a regular paint. Stain-block paint is a primer that will eliminate the difference in colors between the stains and the final coat of new paint.

**Q** I moved into a house that was renovated by the previous owners. I think that they did not prime the woodwork around the doors very well because some knots bled through. I covered the wood with two coats of paint and the knots are still bleeding. What can I do?

**A** Shellac is the standard material to deal with knots. It is not very good as a finish, but is very good as a block. The stain is resin moving its way through the wood and past the coats of paint. You should sand the coats of paint off the wood and, before applying shellac to the surface, apply a small amount of paint cleaner to the knot itself. It will not penetrate the knot very deeply, but enough so that the shellac, when applied, will hold much better. There are some stain-block paints on the market that are, in fact, white shellacs. Make sure that the shellac is less than a year old, and mix it well before applying.

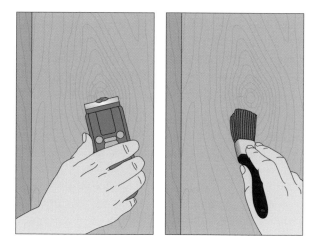

**Q** How do I fill a knothole in my deck railing so that it will last?

**A** You need technique, but you also need the right product for the job. If you use a filler that shrinks, then you will need to apply several coats. If it shrinks too much, it may just fall out of the knothole. If it is not weatherproof, it may soften and swell up, even under a paint job. Why do most wood fillers shrink? Most of them harden by having their water or solvent evaporate. That means there is less mass as it gets harder and it collapses in on itself. Some fillers set hard first, then the water evaporates, hence they don't shrink and they don't swell. Use an exterior wood filler on that deck railing. Now a couple of tips to make a good filler stick even better. Scrape up the smooth knothole sides, and gouge a bit so that the filler can get a mechanical hold on the wood. You could even add nails or screws into the bottom of the knothole so that the filler will go around and grab onto the heads. Good fillers can be sanded or planed and, with pilot holes, nailed or screwed into. You can add a little bit of water-based stain before filling and finish off the color match after it is dry.

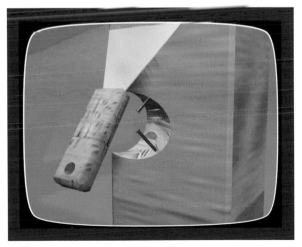

 For more detail, click on "Exteriors" on the home screen of the **CD-ROM.**

**Q** I live in a wooden house that was built in 1815. In the six years I have lived there, I have had to paint the outside of the house three times because the paint keeps peeling off. Am I not using the right paint, or does the problem lie elsewhere?

**A** If the peeling is occurring all across the wood surface, then there is a problem with the paint combinations that you used, or the wood was not primed properly. The result is that the paint is not adhering well. If the peeling is on specific areas of the surface, then it is most likely a moisture problem. Verify that flashings and poor caulking are not letting rainwater behind the paint. Modern insulation has also changed this house. The insulation holds the heat and the siding freezes much more than it did in 1815. If, however, a house is not sealed completely, or at least as well as possible, humidity will escape, and painted areas where the humidity escapes and freezes are going to suffer damage. The obvious areas where humidity would escape would be around window edges, electrical outlets, and wall and floor joints. Examine the areas where the paint is peeling and see if it corresponds to an area inside that may be allowing humidity to pass. If it is an electrical outlet, install a gasket. If it is a window, then make sure the window edges are properly caulked from the inside.

**Q** My outside steps are made of painted wood. During the winter, the steps are considerably slippery. I want to strip the existing paint and apply a new coat. Can the steps be made less slippery?

**A** One of the biggest problems with slippery stairs is the angle at which they are placed. Often the steps are slightly sloped downward. This is to prevent water from collecting at the back of the step. The problem with this is that when it is covered with ice and if you place your foot on the step, it slides forward. If you can, I would suggest changing the angle of the steps. To answer your original question, no, there is not a type of paint on the market that will eliminate the slippery steps. There is, however, a product that will give the step more traction. Remove the existing paint. After applying a new coat of paint, and before it dries, sprinkle some No Slip™ compound. This is a powder that contains both sand and glass. Once the paint dries, it will leave a rough, abrasive surface. It is somewhat difficult to keep clean, but it will provide some much-appreciated traction on the step surface and it works with any paint.

**Q** I recently bought an old house that has a sprayed-on stucco ceiling, complete with small ridges and valleys. I know that the surface must be cleaned before I can paint over it, but how can I clean the ceiling without destroying the stucco pattern?

**A** There are two methods available to you. The first thing that you should do is find out if the stucco is waterproof or not. Put a very small amount of hot water on a cloth and gently rub the stucco surface. Do this in the corner of the ceiling so that it will not be noticeable. If the stucco does not soften, then you will know that it is water-resistant. At this point you can apply some trisodium phosphate (TSP) with a bristle brush (if you want to be more careful, use a paintbrush) to clean the ceiling. If the stucco does soften when you apply the hot water, then you will have to use stain block. This is a very sticky substance that will attach itself to anything—including pollution and nicotine—that has likely built up on the ceiling surface over the years. Over that applying paint will not be a problem.

**Q** I have some ceramic tiles on my bathroom walls. Most of them are beige, with a smaller number of different-colored tiles. I want to keep the beige tiles and paint over the others. Can I paint tiles? If so, what kind of paint should I use?

**A** Yes, you can paint tiles, but that was not always the case. Tiles are so glossy that no paint available can adhere to the surface. However, by using a relatively new super-adherent primer that will, as the name suggests, adhere to difficult surfaces, you can then apply any kind of paint over that. You should be warned that no paint will last forever in the shower area. You will have to repeat the process over time. The ideal paint to apply over the super-adherent primer is a latex-and-acrylic combination paint. It is very durable and can withstand scrubbing without suffering any damage. There are several super-adherent primers on the market. You want one that is specifically designed for ceramic tiles.

**Q** I bought some unfinished, unstained pine furniture. I want to put a finish on the furniture, but I do not want a high-gloss finish. What are my other options, and what is the best method for applying the finish?

**A** The first thing that you must do is test the wood to see what it will look like when you apply the finish. Apply a thin layer of paint thinner across the surface of the wood. This will allow you to see what areas of the wood were not sanded properly. Wood may look well-sanded when you buy it, but this is rarely the case. Before you apply any finish, you must sand the entire piece thoroughly. There are alternatives to a high-gloss finish. There are matte, satin, semigloss, and gloss. What you should be aware of is that the higher the gloss, the better protected the wood will be. You can buy stains that have absolutely no finish. They come in gels and liquids, but both should be applied with a foam brush. Once that has dried, you can apply any type of transparent finish. If the pine furniture does not have a lot of mechanical wear, then the finish you might want to use is tung oil, which will leave a deep oil finish.

**Q** I built a pine bread box for my wife, which I protected with varathane. It has been some time since the varathane was applied but the bread inside the box continues to hold the odor of the varathane. What can I do to eliminate the problem?

**A** If it has been some time since the varathane was applied, then it should be strong enough to be scrubbed. Rub a mixture of baking soda and water over the surface and be sure to get inside all the corners. If possible do it in a warm-to-hot room to help the baking soda soak up the odor. You do not have to heat up the bread box, but warm temperatures will reduce the odors considerably. After that I would keep an open box of baking soda in the bread box the same way many people leave one in their refrigerator.

**Q** I recently built some kitchen cabinets which now have to be painted. I want to make sure the finish is as smooth as possible. Should I use a paint spray gun?

**A** It is possible to achieve a very smooth finish using a spray gun. You should be warned, however, that there is more preparation and work involved when using a spray gun. The first is that the paint has to be a particular thickness and consistency for every brand of spray gun. You will have to discuss the matter with the personnel at the paint store to make sure you have the right combinations. When painting with a brush or roller, usually some newspaper or plastic sheeting on the floor is enough protection. With the gun, you are going to have to cover everything in the room. As careful as one might be with the gun, everything must be covered. If you do use the spray gun it is extremely important to use even strokes in alternating directions. When spraying, keep the gun aimed straight at the wall, and turn it off at the end of every stroke. Keep the gun the same distance from the surface at all times. If not, the paint will not be distributed evenly.

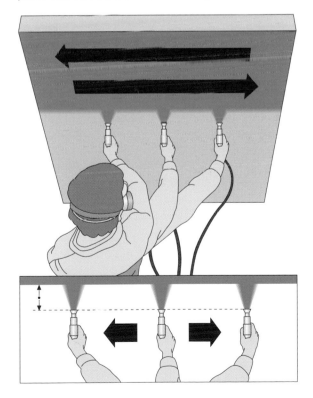

**Q** Last week I installed a new deck in my backyard. How long should I wait until I apply a stain and a water protector to the wood?

**A** The answer to this question depends on two factors. First the type of wood that was installed, and two, the area of the country that you live in. Some pressure-treated woods have wax in them that helps protect the wood from water damage. They can withstand the elements without any protection for a full year. If the wood does not contain wax, the length of time before you should apply the protection is based on the area in which you live. If you are in a dry area, then I would suggest a wait of no longer than two weeks. If you are in a more humid area, then you should delay the application for at least a month, and maybe an entire season. The best way to find out if the wood is ready for water protection is to pour some water on the deck. If the water forms a puddle that remains, then the wood is still well-protected. If the water seeps into the wood, then it needs protection. With regard to staining the wood, if you do not first stain the wood, over time the color of the wood will turn gray. Even if you do stain the wood, it will still turn gray over an extended period. Water sealers with ultraviolet (UV) filters will slow the discoloration of the wood.

**Q** I plan to stain the spindles that form the wall on my backyard deck. Should I use a paintbrush to apply the stain, or is there a better method?

**A** Yes, there is a better method for applying stain to spindles. Using a brush on a flat, even surface is fine, but it will not help spread a stain into wooden spindles very well. There are two items that you can use that will effectively penetrate the wood and do an even job. The first is a wool mitt. It is similar to a winter glove that is formed inside out. The wool fibers are on the outside and the inside is made of rubber. You can easily dip the glove directly into the can of stain and then rub the stain into the spindles. The rubber on the inside of the glove will protect your hand from exposure to the stain. The other item that you can use is a pair of nylon stockings. Again, dip them into the stain and holding either end of the stocking, rub the stain onto and into the grooves on the spindles. Either method works, but the glove is a little easier to handle and cleaner on the hands.

**Q** I have a problem with my nine-year-old pressure-treated deck. It was never painted or stained, and lately when the kids are playing on the deck they are getting splinters. What should I coat the deck with to eliminate the problem?

**A** The great thing about pressure-treated wood is that, in spite of the incessant changes between dampness and dryness, the wood will never rot. The same process of dampness and dryness does, however, cause the wood to check and that is why your kids are getting the splinters. To correct the problem you must first lightly sand the wood to eliminate any existing splinters. The next step is to apply a stain and then a water repellent to the surface. Water repellents are now designed for specific materials, so make sure that you buy the repellent specifically designed for wood. If you want to stain, you have three options. If water repellency is most important to you, do it first and stain after. The stain will not last as long as if it were applied first—it simply cannot soak in as well. If a precise color is more important, apply several coats of light stain to achieve the desired color and then apply water repellent over the stain. If you know that you can get the color in one shot, use a water repellent with stain in it and they will both penetrate well.

**Q** We recently added a cedar deck in our backyard. What would you suggest we apply to the wood to protect it and maintain the natural color of the cedar?

**A** The best protector for wood is a clear sealer. Many people like to varnish their wood. This looks very good, but it requires a lot of maintenance. Make sure that the sealer you buy is one made specifically for cedar with ultraviolet (UV) reflectors. Whether you buy an oil-based or water-based sealer is unimportant. When you start the job, make sure that the surface is clean and dry. Sand the wood lightly before applying the sealer. You will have to add a coat of sealer periodically, but the process will require little preparation. People often apply too many coats to the wood. One or two coats is enough.

**Q** I want to strip the paint off several pieces of furniture but I am worried that this will be expensive. The last time I did a job like this it took a lot of paint stripper. Is there any way to make the stripper go further?

**A** Yes, you can get a lot of mileage out of paint stripper, with a couple of tricks. Spreading it thin is not going to help, it will simply dry out too fast and not do the job at all. Put a collection tray under your work area, so you can collect all the drippings. Let all the mess settle and then pour off the stripper. You can actually recuperate and recycle a good percentage of your original stripper. What has not evaporated will still strip paint. The other trick is to apply it thickly so there are lots of chemicals there to do the job, then cover it all with plastic to prevent evaporation. On small areas, laying plastic kitchen film directly onto the stripper holds all the solvents in where they can take their time to do their job. Preventing evaporation and recycling the liquid saves you money and gets less stripper to remove more paint.

**Q** I have some wrought iron patio chairs. What is the easiest way to remove the paint and refinish them?

**A** The easiest and most effective way to remove paint on wrought iron is to sandblast it off. This is not, obviously, a do-it-yourself job. However, you can take the chairs to an establishment that can do the sandblasting. If you want to do this yourself, you have two options. The first is to remove the paint with grinders and steel brushes. On a flat surface this is a good method, but with patio chairs and their nooks and crannies, it will be difficult to remove the paint. An easier, and more effective method, is to apply a paint-stripper gel that removes paint faster. You can use a liquid paint stripper, and the advantage of using it is that you can recycle it. This will eliminate the need to buy a huge supply. If you use a large bucket over which the stripper is applied, it will collect in the bottom of the bucket. Once it has settled, the paint that has been successfully removed will float to the top. You can skim it off, and underneath is the stripper free of any paint, which can be used again. As far as painting afterward, there are many good paints that you can use, but make sure that you first apply a rustproof primer.

**Q** I have been removing old tiling from the concrete floor in the basement of my 60-year-old house. Underneath the tiles is an old layer of paint. The paint is so old that where it is not still adhering to the floor, it has turned into a powdery substance. Do I have to remove the paint on the floor before I paint again?

**A** You definitely have to remove all of the paint and especially all of the powder. Any paint that you apply can only adhere to the floor if the surface is completely clean. You mentioned that your house is about 60 years old. If the paint that is turning into a powdery substance was applied long ago, there is a good possibility that it is lead-based. If that is the case, you should stay away from the powder. It is very dangerous, particularly for children and pregnant women. Professionals can clean the floor. If you do it yourself, wear full protective gear to remove the excess powder and then build a subfloor. It is much safer than digging and scraping away at the existing paint. It will be a little bit more costly, but there are advantages. Cover the floor with carpeting, put down hardwood floors, or paint the plywood. You will have more options and it will be much safer.

# ROOFING & SIDING

# CHAPTER 9

Roofing and siding are the home's first line of defense against the elements. Generally, their job is to stop the rain and hold back the snow, as well as protecting everything else in the wall against the harsh ultraviolet light of the sun. Yet because roofing and siding are only part of the wall and the roof, they can only do part of the job of protecting us. Indeed, it is rare that roofing or siding are ever insulated, or that they even stop airflow.

In Canada, we rely very heavily on the "rain screen wall" principle for building our walls and roofs. Just as a good rain-coat has holes to keep us from getting hot and sweaty under all that plastic, a good wall is full of holes, too. In fact, when we try to build waterproof walls, the seals almost always leak some day and the walls have trouble drying out. The rain-screen idea is to shed all the water we can, but when some does get in, the wall is both drained and vented so that it can dry out. So attics and walls are vented and the wind and air barriers are located on the inner wall or on the ceiling.

As the questions in this chapter show, this doesn't mean that we don't need to re-point brick or caulk windows or doors. It just means that a well-built wall should have more than just one line of defense.

**Q** The light attached to the soffit above the front door fills with water every time it rains. Excess water then drips down to the porch below. Is this a roofing problem?

**A** It is possible that the water is coming into the roof and is exiting below, where the soffit and the light are located. This is unlikely and I suspect that the water is dripping over the roof and onto the light fixture. If this is the case, there are two possible reasons. First, the water that is supposed to be dripping into the eave is actually dripping between the eave and the siding and is eventually ending up at the light fixture, or the water may be following an electrical wire that runs from the siding to the light. The first thing that you have to do is determine where the water is coming from and how it is reaching the light fixture. A simple trick to find the answer to this question is to take some colored chalk and spread it on the bottom side of the soffit around the light fixture. After the next rainfall investigate the chalk. If the chalk has not been disturbed at all, then the water leakage is coming from the inside. If some of the chalk is missing, then it will leave a clear path and indicate where the water is coming from. If the water is dripping between the eave and the siding, a simple drip-edge flashing at the edge of the roof should solve the problem. Another possibility is to apply a coat of caulking around the top of the light fixture that will create a water barrier. It will not prevent the water from reaching the light fixture, but it will prevent it from entering it.

**Q** My aluminum eaves constantly leak at the seams. I have tried to seal the seams with a variety of products, but nothing seems to help. What can I do?

**A** The problem with aluminum is that it expands and contracts with the changing weather. There is nothing that can be done about that, other than changing the eaves themselves. The problem, however, may lie in the type of sealant you are using on the seams. If your eaves are expanding and contracting, then you should use a sealant that also expands and contracts. The best one to use is polyurethane caulking, which is designed for roof flashings and moves with weather changes. Scrape the aluminum very clean before applying the sealant.

**Q** My house has a poured concrete foundation with brick walls on top. Every time there is a strong rain-storm, water enters the house at the exact point where the foundation and the brick meet. What is the best way to seal the wall?

**A** A properly built brick wall can take a lot of leakage around the brick, without letting any water into the house. The air space behind the brick is designed to let water run down the inside face of the brick. With building paper against the wall on the other side of the air space, any water that manages to get across to the wall will also flow to the bottom. Weep holes—missing mortar in the vertical joint of about every fifth brick on the bottom row—allow the water to then flow out-doors. These holes also allow air to dry out the cavity. This system is based on the "rain screen wall" principle *(see page 155)*. Properly built, there is no need for any sealing or waterproofing of the brick. Make sure that you do not seal the weep holes. Check that the flashings around the windows are properly caulked and that there are no signifi-cant cracks in the mortar.

**Q** I have an extension to my house with a deck on top that acts as a roof. But the deck does not slope away from the house, so every time it rains, the deck fills with a puddle in its center. I have heard that I can build a slope on the deck using thin-set mortar and acrylic milk. Is this possible?

**A** I would not suggest using the thin-set mortar for the simple reason that it does not react well to winter freezing and will crack with just a little bit of movement. If you do want to change the slope of the deck, perhaps the best way is to install tapered layers of rigid foam insulation over which you can put a waterproof membrane. It is a tedious job, but it will work. The other possibility is that if all the water is concentrating in the center of the deck, perhaps installing a drain there will allow you to avoid the tedious task of correcting the slope. The problem will be finding a route for the drain pipe without going through the middle of the room below. If the drain pipe enters the heated portion of the house, cover it thoroughly with insulation and a well-sealed vapor barrier.

**Q** I have a flat tar-and-gravel roof above my garage. I have experienced numerous leaks from the roof into the garage. I sealed all the cracks that I could find on the roof, but the problem persists. What can I do?

**A** The most common source of all roof leaks are unsealed or corroded flashings, joints between two roofs, or penetrations through the roof. Flat-top roofs add the problem of backed-up or standing water. If something stops the flow of water off the roof, the water can back up and even rise up over the flashing. Snow and ice cause a lot of backing up on flat-top roofs and should be controlled. If it is leaking when it is warm, and you have tackled all the obvious cracks, check the flatness and slope of the roof. Over the years, roofs tend to move with the rest of the house. Often a section on the roof surface will sag and will no longer have the elevation or slope for water to drain off. If water collects and sits in any spot, it will eventually weaken the membrane at that point. Check the roof on a rainy day and see if there are any puddles. These points will have to be raised from underneath to allow the water to run off. Eventually you will have to redo the roof.

**Q** I caulk all my windows regularly but I still get water leaks during big rainstorms. Is there anything wrong with the wall?

**A** Walls that rely solely on caulking to keep them watertight have trouble with heavy rain. These walls try to seal out the water, but the caulking always ages and requires maintenance. A wall system that works best has three lines of defense against water penetration. All together we call it a "rain screen" wall. The first line of defense is brick or other siding. This is not totally waterproof. In fact, if you look at brick-veneer walls they have holes at the bottom; vinyl or aluminum siding has holes under every row of siding. These holes serve as vent holes to let air in and out behind the siding to help keep it dry. They also let the air in so that the wind literally blows on both sides of the brick, which means there is little or no wind force to drive water through the brick. The second line of defense is an air space and then a membrane against the wall that sheds water, like building paper. Most of the water that does get past the siding will flow down the back side of the siding. The little that gets across the air space flows down the membrane. And the bottom of the wall is always flashed and drained to the outside. The third line of defense is an air barrier somewhere in the wall that stops the wind so it will not blow into the house. A properly built rain-screen wall is almost always a trouble-free wall.

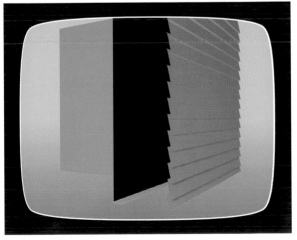

 For more detail, click on "Walls" on the home screen of the CD-ROM.

**Q** Every time a heavy rain blows on the east side of my two-story brick house, water enters through the wall, runs along a steel I beam connecting the first and the second floor, and drips through the ceiling onto my living room floors. How is the water entering the house and how do I fix it?

**A** There are several reasons why water may be entering the house. Water is getting behind the brick wall and running along the beam to a point where it eventually drips down. It is possible that the water is entering under the soffit or it is entering the wall through poorly sealed window frames or door attachments. Once it has entered, it is either being drawn toward the inside wall by poorly positioned metal ties that hold the brick wall parallel to the inside wall, or the brick wall is touching the inside wall and the water is seeping through. If the windows and doors are tightly sealed, you should add a wood trim to the top of the soffit to stop any water from entering. The air holes found at the bottom of all brick walls may also be blocked. The air holes serve a dual purpose: Firstly, they allow excess water that enters the space between the brick wall and the inside wall to drain outside, and they also force pressure on the inside of the brick wall. If water—or air—is entering through cracks in the wall, the air pressure will push back away water trying to get inside. If none of these solutions work, there are two other possibilities. One is to open the brick wall at the end of that I beam and be sure that it is insulated and watertight. The other option is to install some aluminum siding over the brick wall. The brick wall may no longer be exposed, but if properly installed the siding will eliminate the problem immediately.

**Q** My house has an addition that was constructed with a flat roof. Years ago, we had a leak from the flat roof that forced me to install a rubber membrane, with the result that the roof is not perfectly flat anymore. Water collects where there are dips and valleys. Is there anything I can do to eliminate the dips and valleys, or must I install a slanted roof to correct the problem?

**A** Standing water on the roof surface should be eliminated, or it will bring nothing but trouble. The development of low spots that collect water is an indication that there is not enough structural support for the type of roof decking that was used. Because you have a good rubberized membrane on top, you will want to tackle the problem from the bottom. Open up the ceiling below and add cross bracing to the structure to level out the roof deck. If you decide to do this, start with one small hole in the ceiling below the worst depression. Inspect the roof deck to see that it is not simply sagging or rotten. If it is rotten, you cannot tackle the problem from below. If it is sound, then proceed. If you have to rebuild the entire roof, use good materials and be sure that the new roof is built high enough above the walls to permit good insulation and good ventilation.

**Q** Why do some houses have ice dams on the roof and others do not?

**A** Ice dams develop when snow is on the roof, outdoor temperatures are only slightly below freezing, and there is spot or generalized heat loss from the house into the attic/roof section of your house (see page 158). The heat melts the bottom of the snow pack, the melted snow runs down the roof until it gets to the overhang of the roof. Without the heat from the house, the water freezes, creating an ice dam. The solution lies in finding a way to keep the roof cold whenever it is cold outdoors. The snow will either melt and run off the roof, or stay put. Ventilation is the key. Anywhere insulation touches the roof, the ventilation cannot keep the roof frozen and heat will flow through the insulation to melt the snow. Complicated roofs have more problems because the structure tends to block the cold ventilation airflow. Provide continuous airflow to the underside of the roof and you will have no more ice.

**Q** Last year I installed a new roof on my 40-year-old house. In doing so, I installed two new soffit vents so that the roof now has four vents. I was having—and continue to have—problems with ice dams forming. Are the vents not doing the trick, and what can I do to correct the problem?

**A** The problem with some older houses is that attic insulation often comes into direct contact with the roof. There may be soffit vents in place, and ventilation directly above the attic insulation, but that one small area of insulation is coming in contact with the roof. The area in question is where the attic floor, the sloping roof, and the house siding all connect. That one small area becomes much warmer than the rest of the roof. It melts the snow, and as it drips further down, the roof becomes colder again, and the water turns into ice, forming the dams. If you installed two new soffit vents, that will improve overall ventilation, but it will not tackle the problem of the ice dams. What you need to do is install some baffles in that problem area to allow a smooth and complete flow of air between the soffits and the attic. This should eliminate or reduce the ice dam.

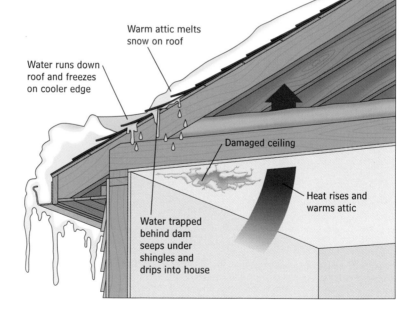

Warm attic melts snow on roof

Water runs down roof and freezes on cooler edge

Damaged ceiling

Heat rises and warms attic

Water trapped behind dam seeps under shingles and drips into house

**Q** I would like to have a ridge vent installed on my roof. Is it a do-it-yourself job, and if so, how do I install one?

**A** The only reason that this should not be a do-it-yourself job is if you have a fear of heights and will be uncomfortable working on the roof. If not, then yes, you can install a ridge vent yourself. As the name implies, a ridge vent rests on the spine of a double-sloped roof and allows roof ventilation from between pairs of roof joists. Ridge vents are required for cathedral ceilings. To install a ridge vent, the first task required is to remove the shingles at the ridge of the roof, and saw off about 5 cm (2 in.) of the roof deck on either side of the ridge. This will be the space through which air can flow and over which the ridge vent will be placed. Traditional ridge vents have the problem of snow accumulation. Newer models of ridge vent on the market have improved designs that prevent snow accumulation, such as a sealed ridge vent that feeds two or three passive vent stacks that stand high above the snow.

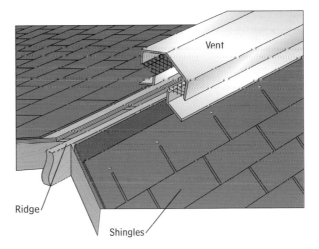

Vent

Ridge

Shingles

**Q** There are cracked mortar joints on the outside of my chimney. Can I use polyurethane to fill the cracks?

**A** Yes, you can fill the cracks with polyurethane specifically designed for concrete. However you can do this only if the cracks on your chimney are minor. If the brick is actually falling out of the mortar, you will have to rejoint the mortar. You may also have to replace the chimney liner inside the chimney chute. If it is damaged, it can lead to deterioration of the bricks.

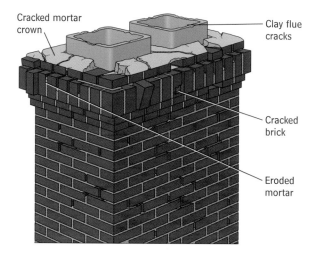

Cracked mortar crown

Clay flue cracks

Cracked brick

Eroded mortar

**Q** I changed my standard brick fireplace to a gas one. I installed a liner on the inside of the chimney, but I am finding condensation between the liner and the chimney wall. It does not matter if it rains, or snows, or is dry, there is always condensation. Why has the liner not helped?

**A** Too much cold air at the top of the chimney has created condensation. Older houses typically had the fireplace and the chimney in the middle of the house. This meant that any heat loss through the masonry would remain in the house. Newer houses have the fireplace and chimney on the outside walls, so some heat will exit the masonry and stay in the house, but some will leave the house through the outside wall. The end result is condensation. This happens with all new houses, but there must be something else happening that is leading to the amount of condensation you describe. My guess is that the liner is not properly sealed at the top and bottom of the chimney. If that is the case, cold air is entering the space between the liner and the chimney wall from above, and moist household air is entering from the bottom. If you seal the area where the liner and chimney meet, you should stop the condensation.

**Q** How can I patch concrete steps so that the concrete won't chip and break off every spring?

**A** Concrete has a tough time outdoors because of a combination of frost and deicing compounds. You should start by hammering and brushing off all the loose material. Then dampen the concrete. You don't want any standing water, which would dilute the new coatings, but if the concrete is too dry, it will draw the water out of the new material. For best adhesion, apply a bonding agent or primer made specifically for concrete. Simply paint it on. Be ready to work quickly, as you should apply the patch after the bonding agent gets tacky but before it gets dry. If your cement patch comes with a mention on the bag that it is "polymer modified," then simply mix with water and apply according to the instructions on the bag. If it is not polymer modified, use the bonding agent rather than water to mix the patch material. Do not water the patch with a hose as it will rinse off the polymers, rather cover it all with a plastic sheet to prevent evaporation. Leave it set for three days.

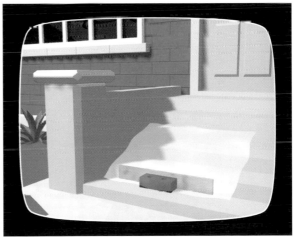

 For more detail, click on "Exteriors" on the home screen of the CD-ROM.

**Q** I want to install new shingles on my roof. Which ones are the best to use, fiberglass or felt-based asphalt shingles? And is there any difference between three-tab and one-piece shingles?

**A** Both the standard three-tab shingle and the longer one-piece shingle are good. In terms of which will last longer, the difference is not in the shingle's length but its thickness. Obviously the thicker the shingle, the more durable it will be. The difference between the two is strictly a question of design. With regard to fiberglass or felt-based shingles, they are relatively new in Canada and the jury is still out on their long-term success in our climate. If you choose to install any non-standard shingles, I would ask around for references from contractors and homeowners. Inquire if they have had any problems. If you live in a windy area, try interlocking shingles. Each shingle has clips on its underside that lock into place with the shingle below. As you know, strong wind is one of the greatest enemies of a shingle roof. This type of shingle will remain in place even when the wind is strong.

**Q** I have recently noticed some green mold on my shingled roof. What should I do to remove it, and what can I do to prevent its return?

**A** You can easily scrape off the existing mold and afterward apply a standard cleaner to remove any excess. There are products on the market that can prevent mold from ever returning. Some are thin strips of zinc that slide into place under the shingles. You should install these shingle shields at or near the top of the roof, extending its entire length. It is only necessary to install one complete strip—not several layers. What the shingle shields do is release a microscopic amount of zinc every time it rains. It will run down and cover all the shingles, protecting them from mold. The amount of zinc released will prevent any return of the mold, but it is not powerful enough to do any damage to the shingles themselves.

**Q** I want to lay new asphalt shingles on my roof. How far should the shingles overhang the edge of the roof?

**A** They should not overhang more than 2.5 cm (1 in.). Any distance more and the shingles will break off with the weight of snow and ice in the winter. What you do want on the edge of the roof is something called a drip-edge. When rain water or melted snow runs off the last shingle, most of it will drop to the ground because of gravity. Some will, however, work its way under the last shingle. If there is enough water there it will soak into the roof deck and may cause some damage. A drip-edge is a long strip of aluminum that sits underneath the last shingle. When excess water works its way up the inside of the last shingle, it will be blocked by the drip-edge. A simple trick that will prolong the life of the house!

**Q** When I try cleaning the siding on my house, I always end up with ghostlike dirty streaks running vertically up the outside wall. What am I doing wrong?

**A** You are cleaning from the top down! While that appears to be the logical thing to do, the soapy dirt that flows down over the still-dirty wall below tends to create streaks. Always clean exterior walls from the bottom up. Work on the shaded side of the house and move fast enough to keep the whole area you are working on completely wet until you have reached the eaves at the top. Dirty water flowing over the clean surface below won't have streaks, and keeping the wall wet until it is all clean and rinsed keeps any dirt from drying on the surface before reaching the ground.

**Q** I have made several attempts to clean the aluminum siding on my backyard workshed, without much luck. Is there a special trick to cleaning aluminum?

**A** For general cleaning of aluminum, it is best to use a mild detergent and water. For detergent, choose the same type of soap that you would use to clean your car. A more ambitious method is to buy or rent a power hose. If the shed is in your backyard, make sure that the detergent used is biodegradable. For dirt and stains that can not be cleaned with water and soap, try using some trisodium phosphate (TSP) and water. If there is any moss on the siding, add some bleach to the TSP. If none of these methods works, there are products that are designed to prepare aluminum and vinyl sidings for painting.

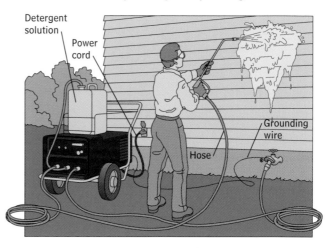

Detergent solution
Power cord
Grounding wire
Hose

**Q** What is the best way to repair rotten wooden lap siding?

**A** There is no way to repair large areas of rotten wood; it will simply have to be replaced. If you can see the nails that are holding the siding to the house, pull them out or drive them in with a nail set. Sometimes it is difficult to see all the nails if the siding is covered with several coats of paint. If this is the case, pull up the siding with a pry bar or shims until the piece pulls free. It is important to replace the piece of siding with a piece of the same type of wood. Take the rotten piece to a hardware store or your local lumberyard if you are not sure what type it is. Prime the new wood on all sides with a sealer before installation. It can then be cut, put into place, and nailed in.

**Q** The silicone caulking on the aluminum siding of my house needs to be replaced. What is the best way to remove it, and what kind of caulking should replace it?

**A** The first thing to do is mechanically remove the silicone caulking using a knife or scraper. You should be able to remove most of it this way. Use a silicone caulking stripper to remove the rest. Be very careful using the stripper, as it may remove some of the paint on the aluminum siding. You must use caulking stripper, however, because it is essential that all of the caulking is removed—silicone caulking is very popular because nothing will stick to it, including more of it. If the caulking you want to remove is not removed completely, the new silicone caulking will not hold and you will have leaks. It is for this reason that I always recommend polyurethane caulking. As a sealant, it works as well as, if not better than, silicone caulking, and if you need to retouch the job, the new caulking will adhere to the old.

**Q** Can I paint my wooden lap siding with a brush or a roller?

**A** You can use a brush or a roller, but it will be difficult. The best tools to apply paint to lap siding are spray guns and pad applicators. The pad applicator is ideal for lap siding because it can reach under the laps. Downward strokes with the pad applicator allow paint to penetrate lap-siding grooves. A spray gun is also useful when painting lap siding because it can easily cover all surfaces on lap siding, provided the gun is used properly. If you choose the spray gun method, three light coats of paint should be applied from different angles. First spray from below at a 45° angle, making sure the paint penetrates under the laps. The second coat should be directed downward at a 45° angle, and the third should be sprayed directly on the lap siding. Do not try to spray in direct sunlight; the paint may dry before it hits the wall.

**Q** I want to change the color of the vinyl siding on my house with a coat of paint. What kind of paint should I be using, and is there any special method to applying it?

**A** As is the case before painting any type of material, the surface must first be washed. However, it is extremely important to use a cleaner that is designed specifically for vinyl and aluminum siding. There are several good brands of paint on the market, but what is most important is to choose a paint that is labeled all-acrylic. As you know, vinyl expands and contracts more than most other sidings. If the paint applied over the vinyl siding cannot expand and contract as much (or at the same rate), it will not adhere and will peel and chip off over a short period of time. An all-acrylic paint will move with the vinyl surface. You will, however, need to apply at least two thin coats, maybe more, as thick coats of all-acrylic paint will not hold well on vinyl siding.

**Q** We are thinking about moving to an area in British Columbia that has few brick houses but many stucco siding houses. I was told that new acrylic stucco siding, as opposed to wood or aluminum siding, requires little maintenance. This sounds a little fishy to me. What is the truth?

**A** From the Prairies west there are few brick-sided houses for two reasons: Firstly, brick structures are expensive to build and, secondly, stucco-sided houses are excellent for blocking wind, something that plagues Prairie winters. Unless you seriously damage the stucco siding, it requires little maintenance. Regardless what kind of siding you build with, periodic cleaning is required. Acrylic stucco is much easier to clean than concrete-based stucco but does not allow the wall to dry if water gets behind the stucco, which can cause damage in the wall in the damp coastal climate. The problem that you are likely to encounter on the West Coast is a buildup of moss, which you will have to clean off on a regular basis. When comparing stucco to aluminum or wood siding, there is one great difference: stucco will withstand abuse from a tree better than the others because it will not dent at all.

**Q** **The north wall in our house is unusually cold yet it is full of insulation. What's wrong and what can I do to increase the heat?**

**A** You may have a problem called thermal bridging but we need to see inside the wall to fully understand it. When it gets cold outside, the insulation in the wall cavity does a good job of keeping out the cold, but the uninsulated wood framing allows a lot of heat to escape, as wood is not a very good insulator. All this heat loss through the studs means that the winter cold is moving *in* through the same path. Besides making the wall cold, moisture can collect on the coldest spots over the studs, and trap dust from the air—resulting in dirty stripes on the wall. If it gets cold enough to cause serious condensation, then mold can start to grow. You may not realize it but more than 20 percent of our walls consist of wood framing, not insulation. That is the equivalent of a hole in every home the size of a garage door that is left uninsulated. Putting rigid foam insulation over the wall, inside or out, will insulate the wood as well as the wall, blocking the heat loss. If you are residing in the house, insulate from the outside. Otherwise simply put rigid foam insulation over the wallpaper on the inside and put new drywall over it. A few adjustments to the window frame and electrical boxes and your north wall will be considerably warmer.

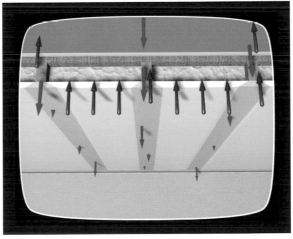

 For more detail, click on "Walls" on the home screen of the CD-ROM.

# JON'S TOOLBOX

# CHAPTER 10

No matter how we divide up a house, there are always things that don't fit neatly into our categories, a bit like those odd tools that don't quite fit with our pliers, screwdrivers, or hammers. But that doesn't mean that the things I have put into this toolbox are not important. Quite the contrary. They are the glue which will hold your home renovation projects together.

Knowing how to choose your tools and products can be as important as the techniques to use them. And upgrading and improving your tool skills are among the trade secrets of the pros. Armed with a better knowledge of your tools and how to use them, your job will be neater, more professional, and will take half the time.

Stiff paintbrushes? Marred workpieces? Jammed caulking guns? In this chapter you will find valuable hints and tips on caulking, fireplaces, kitchen countertops, adhesives, paints—even when and how to hire a professional. Is your scorched kitchen countertop beyond repair? Want to convert your dormant fireplace into a working one? Should I leave it to the pros? Read on and find out.

**Q** I have an arborite kitchen countertop over which I would like to apply more arborite. Do I have to remove the existing arborite or can I just put the new over the old?

**A** Both methods can be used to improve your kitchen countertop. If you simply put new arborite over the old, the new arborite will not stick well to the old because of its glossy surface. Take a circular sander and rough up the surface. This will allow the contact cement to bond with the surface. If you choose to remove the existing arborite first, use a hot air gun or an iron to soften the glue and you can work a spatula under the arborite to lift it off the counter.

**Q** Do laminate countertops require any maintenance?

**A** There are some things that can—and should—be done to plastic laminate countertops. As convenient as they are, laminate countertops are susceptible to stains. Regular everyday stains can be absorbed by wiping with a damp brush or rag with some mild detergent. Stronger stains such as ink and dyes can be removed using a soft rag and alcohol or bleach. It is important to use a soft rag or brush; an abrasive rag or brush will scour the surface. It is also important to keep the surface edges as dry as possible. If moisture gets under the edges, the laminate will pull back from the countertop. If this happens, apply more contact cement and glue the plastic back into place.

**Q** I accidentally burned my laminate kitchen countertop with a hot frying pan. Is there any way to repair it without replacing the entire countertop?

**A** Very minor burns in laminate countertops can be scraped clean, but major burns require some surgery. I would never try to repair a hot frying pan burn, but rather I would cut a hole in the counter, removing the burned area, and replace it with a ceramic tile or wood cutting block. The best thing about this solution is that the tile or cutting block will in all likelihood be located exactly where the next hot frying pan is going to land, avoiding future burns.

**Q** I am going to caulk my windows for the winter. Are there any special caulking techniques I should know about?

**A** I am glad you asked, as most people just assume they know how. Cutting the end of the tube at 45°, as recommended by most caulking manufacturers, is not the best idea. It is better to cut it straight across. A tube cut at 45° will produce a nice looking bead, but it will not force the caulking hard enough into the crack. Also, laying the bead gently on the surface won't help it to stick. You should hold the caulking gun perpendicular to the surface to be caulked so the compound is forced into place as you move the gun along. When filling a hole, you should put a backer rod into the bottom of the hole so that the caulking can be forced into the crack and pushed up against both sides. A caulking bead should not be more than 9 mm ($^3/_8$ in.) thick and 12 mm ($^1/_2$ in.) wide. If you are caulking a hairline crack in a concrete wall, chisel out a groove of this size right over the crack. Don't simply fill the crack with caulking; if it sticks to both sides and the bottom it will have no stretching ability if the crack moves again. The trick is to put masking tape into the bottom of the groove, covering up the crack, then caulk. The caulking will stick to the two sides of the groove but not to the bottom. If the crack moves again, you have a full 12 mm ($^1/_2$ in.) of material available for stretching.

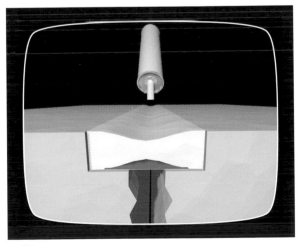

 For more detail, click on "Jon's Toolbox" on the home screen of the CD–ROM.

**Q** I want to fix a broken lamp-shade, but no glue seems to work on hard plastic. Is there any way to salvage it?

**A** Hard plastic has always been a real challenge for the glue manufacturers but they have finally solved the problem by using two glues to get the job done. Rigid plastic adhesive consists of two parts: a primer and the glue itself. The primer is a very thin liquid that has the ability to stick to the smooth surface of plastic. First prepare the surfaces to be glued. Because rigid plastic adhesive will not fill gaps, the two surfaces have to fit perfectly together. The strength of rigid plastic adhesive is proportional to the surface area being glued, so narrow edges won't hold as well as overlapped pieces of plastic. Apply the primer to both surfaces to be glued together. Be prepared to work quickly, as the primer dries within a minute. Next apply the glue to only one surface, and put the pieces together. There is no need of clamping; the beauty of rigid plastic adhesive is that you only need to hold it together for 20 seconds, then it will hold itself. Don't test it yet, as it takes about 12 hours to cure properly. Then your lamp should be as good as new.

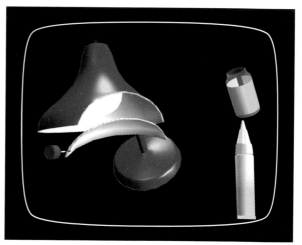

 For more detail, click on "Jon's Toolbox" on the home screen of the CD-ROM.

**Q** How do you prevent glue from hardening too quickly, and how do you get glue into small spaces?

**A** Glues set by many different mechanisms. Some set by heat, some with pressure, some by evaporation of solvents. Silicone and polyurethane set by reacting with moisture in the air. If your glue sets by evaporation, stay away from air currents and heat. You can also buy glues specially formulated to set quickly or slowly. Quick-setting glues are best for hard-to-clamp objects, slow glues are best for hard-to-assemble projects. To answer the second part of your question, to apply glue to small nooks and crannies you can either dab some glue on the end of a toothpick or shoot glue out of a plastic glue syringe found in most hardware and hobby stores.

**Q** I have used contact cement for years but now I see a water-based contact cement in the stores. Is this as strong as the old type?

**A** We tend to think that water-based products are inferior to the old solvent-based stand-bys, but in the case of solvent-free, water-based contact cement, the new version is really an improvement. First, it is thinner, so although it sells for more, it costs less per square meter/square foot. It is not flammable and has no bothersome odors. It actually sticks as well as if not better than standard contact cement in all adhesion tests and supports considerably higher temperatures before delaminating. On top of all that, it even changes color to let you know it is ready to join the two pieces together. Best of all, once ready, you can wait up to 48 hours before joining the pieces together. Try it; you'll never go back.

**Q** I am thinking of converting my decorative fireplace into a working one. What are the standard safety precautions for a fireplace?

**A** The first precaution is a fire extinguisher. Make sure you have one in the room that has the fireplace, and make sure everyone in the house is aware of its location and how to use it. Make sure that the wood you burn in the fireplace does not contain any chemicals or plastics. This will produce toxic fumes and dangerously large flames. Make sure that any flammable household items such as furniture, rugs, and pillows, are at least 90 cm (3 ft) away from the fireplace edge. The flue should be checked for creosote buildup regularly and a professional chimney cleaner should be hired annually. Last, it would be wise to check with city officials because there are municipal laws that govern how a fireplace should be maintained and what materials are allowable. The safest and most energy-efficient tactic is to install a fireplace insert—a safe, manufactured fireplace that slides inside your existing fireplace.

**Q** We have a floor-to-ceiling fireplace made of rock. Over the years, the rock has been discolored from escaping smoke. I want to know if it can be cleaned, and if there is any danger involved?

**A** With a little bit of work and prudence, yes, it can be cleaned. The best material and method to use is a bristle brush and muriatic acid. Although a very effective cleaning agent, muriatic acid is a very dangerous product to use, so it is imperative to wear rubber gloves with a long-sleeved shirt, goggles, and a mask. The bristle brush is necessary to clean the surface properly. Unfortunately, this results in splattering. Therefore the protective equipment is an absolute must. It is also important to make sure that the floor surrounding the wall is covered, and that the room is well ventilated.

**Q** I would like to undertake some of the renovation of my house myself, but I realize that some jobs are best left to the pros. When should I hire someone rather than taking on a job myself?

**A** Probably the three most important questions to ask yourself are: Do you have the skills to do the job at hand? Be honest, because you want to do a good job. Second, do you have the time to do this job? It will probably take a bit longer than you think. Third, do you enjoy doing your own renovation work? Renovation can be stressful work, and if you don't enjoy it, having a professional renovation contractor responsible for the work can make the project more satisfying. Also, anytime the job involves major plumbing, electricity, heating, or the structure of the house, you really want to think twice about doing it yourself—or even hiring just anybody. Most provinces require permits for this work, as well many require specially licensed workers. Remember that coordination and supervision of different specialized trades are an important part of a professional renovator's job. He has more influence over subtrades than you do and professional coordination could make the difference between satisfaction and frustration.

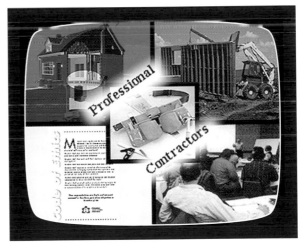

 For more detail, click on "Jon's Toolbox" on the home screen of the CD–ROM.

**Q** I have always put wood blocks between my clamps and workpieces to prevent marking the wood. I see that newer clamps have rubber protectors for this purpose that make assembly much easier. Can I buy these protectors for my old clamps?

**A** Not to my knowledge, but you are right that it would be nice to have these rubber caps in all your clamps. I have found two ways to accomplish this. Find a hard rubber or soft plastic material. You want something that does not leave color marks, so steer clear of black rubber. Polyurethane adhesive is able to glue rubber and plastic to metal. If your caps are soft enough to spread when clamped, use a softer polyurethane caulking as the adhesive. The longest-lasting caps will be ones that are grooved to fit over the metal face, giving mechanical resistance to slip so the glue has less to do. The second technique is to simply put a blob of polyurethane caulking over the face of the clamp and down around the edges. Let it set and then cut the face flat and about 3 mm ($1/8$ in.) thick.

**Q** How do I protect wood when it is placed in a vise?

**A** There are some vises available that come with protective pads. Usually made from a piece of thick rubber or softwood, the pads do not ease the pressure on the object in the vise, but they will not mark the object the way a vise's metal edge sometimes does. If you own a vise that does not have protective pads, you can easily make some. Cut two pieces of 18 mm ($3/4$ in.) thick wood equal in size to the vise jaws. Glue a magnetic strip onto the edges of the wood. The magnets will hold the cushion in place, and if needed they can be easily removed. Another option is to make an L-shaped lip by screwing two pieces of wood together perpendicular to each other. The pieces can then rest on top and over the side of the vise's jaws. Both methods will protect the objects placed in the vise, and give you access to the metal vise when you need it.

**Q** How can I increase the life of a paintbrush?

**A** There are several precautions you can take while painting and after painting that will increase the life of a paintbrush. Before you begin painting, apply masking tape over the end of the brush where the bristles meet the handle. Allow about 12 mm ($^1/_2$ in.) of bristle coverage. Paint will not penetrate the ends of the bristles, which are very difficult to clean. When you do clean the brush, remove the masking tape. When you are finished painting, clean the brush as soon as possible. The longer you wait, the harder the paint becomes, making cleaning difficult. Latex paint is the easiest to work with, as it washes out with water. Oil paint has to be cleaned with paint thinner or turpentine. If you finish a coat of oil paint and plan to apply another coat the following day, there is no need to clean the brush. Wrap the brush in foil or plastic and place it in the freezer. Cold temperature prevents oil paint from hardening. Make sure that you allow the brush to thaw for about 45 minutes before you resume painting.

**Q** I've chosen a nice, dark decor paint for my dining room, but it doesn't seem to cover the color of the wall underneath. I've done four coats and I'm still not happy with the results. What am I doing wrong?

**A** In order to achieve the deep, rich colors in decor paint, it is necessary to leave the white pigment out of the paint. Yet it is this white base pigment that gives the paint its ability to hide what was on the wall before. The solution? Always use a top-quality primer paint before a color decor paint. In fact, you can even tint the primer slightly in the direction of the final coat. The primer will completely cover what was there before and present an even surface that is easy to cover with the decor paint. Using this trick, you will get results with one, or at most, two coats of decor paint.

# Glossary

**Air barrier** An assembly of construction elements that, together as a system, block air from moving through the building envelope. *See* Vapor barrier.

**Alkyd** A synthetic resin paint base that is similar to linseed oil.

**Baseboard** A horizontal molding found at the base of a wall.

**Bearing wall** A wall that supports the weight of a house. *See* Nonbearing wall.

**Bedding** Tapping a tile or floor piece with adhesive to align it with adjoining tiles or floor pieces.

**Bonding** Adhering one material to another, such as a tile and glue.

**Casing** Decorative trim found around a door or window.

**Caulk** Material used to create a watertight seal for windows, siding, and bathtubs.

**Cellulose insulation** A type of insulation using cellulose as its primary ingredient.

**Cementious paint** Paint that contains a small amount of cement to provide a rough texture and adhesive capabilities.

**Circuit breaker** A safety switch that cuts electrical power automatically when the current exceeds the normal amount.

**Cladding** A generic name given to exterior wall coverings, including aluminum siding and brick.

**Concrete** A mixture of portland cement, gravel, sand, and water. *See* Portland cement.

**Condensation** The process whereby water vapor turns to liquid.

**Corner bead** A metal strip that provides protection to a plaster or drywall corner.

**Coupling** A fitting that attaches two pieces of straight pipe.

**Crawl space** A small space underneath the first floor of a house; typically not high enough for one to stand erect.

**Damper** A valve that opens and closes a fireplace chimney.

**Deck** An outdoor porch typically made of wood.

**Draft** An uncontrolled flow of air in or out of a house.

**Drip-cap flashing** Z-shaped flashing located over the tops of windows and doors designed to shed water from both inside and outside the cladding over and beyond the window frame on the outside.

**Drywall** Interior finish wall made of plaster, gypsum, or plywood.

**Eave flashing** A flashing designed to prevent leaks from ice dams. *See* Ice dam.

**Eaves** The overhang of a house's roof that shelters the wall and windows below.

**Extruded polystyrene insulation** A type of rigid foam insulation commonly sold under the trade name Styrofoam.

**Flashing** Plastic or metal fixture designed to prevent water leaks on windowsills and roofs.

**Flux** A deoxidation agent used to prepare copper pipes for soldering.

**Footing** The part of a house's foundation that sits on the soil.

**Forced air system** A central heating system that uses warm air to heat a house.

**Foundation** The part of a house that transfers the weight of the house to the earth.

**Frost line** The maximum depth below the surface that soil will freeze. Usually 1.2 m (4 ft).

**Gasket** An elastic strip that forms a seal between two metal or plastic pieces.

**Grade** The level where the top of the soil contacts the foundation. Sometimes used to refer to the slope of the soil with respect to water runoff.

**Ground fault circuit interrupter (GFCI)** An electrical safety device designed to prevent electric shocks in areas of high moisture.

**Grounding wire** An electrical wire that grounds metal appliances to the earth, typically green in color.

**Grout** Thin mortar used to fill in between tiles.

**Heat pump** An appliance that moves heat from one place to another to either heat or cool the house.

**Humidifier** An appliance that adds vapor to a house and reduce the dryness in the air.

**I beam** A structural steel beam used in house construction.

**Ice dam** A ridge of ice that develops at the edge of a roof due to improper ventilation.

**Ice lens** A flat plate of ice that forms in wet clay soil under freezing temperatures and expands in the direction of heat loss.

**Insulation** A material resistant to heat flow installed in a house to prevent heat loss.

**Joist** A horizontal wooden framing that supports the weight of plywood flooring.

**Latex paint** A paint made from water-based latex.

**Mineral spirits** A petroleum-based solvent used as a general cleaner.

**Moisture barrier** Aluminum or plastic sheeting that blocks the passage of water. Also known as a vapor barrier.

**Muriatic acid** A chemical cleaning agent used to clean concrete.

**Nonbearing wall** A wall that does not support the weight of the ceiling above. *See* Bearing wall.

**O-ring** A rubber ring that prevents leaking in the stem of a faucet.

**Parging** A thick, cement-based coating used to cover concrete or masonry for a smooth finish.

**Parquet** Wood flooring laid out in blocks or squares.

**Partition wall** A non-bearing wall that divides a room into two.

**Pipe-joint compound** A sealant applied to threaded pipe fittings.

**Plaster** A combination of lime, sand, and water used to repair walls and ceilings.

**Plywood** Manufactured wood panels made of at least three layers of veneer.

**Portland cement** A water-resistant cement composed of lime, silica, and alumina.

**Pressure-balancing valve** A plumbing valve used for showers which maintains a preset temperature to counteract pressure fluctuations in the plumbing system.

**Primer** A base layer of paint with concealing and adhesive qualities.

**Quarter-round molding** Wood or plastic molding in the shape of a quarter circle used as the final trim piece on baseboards.

**Rafter** A framing member in house construction that supports the weight of the roof.

**Rain-screen wall** A wall design that incorporates a complete air-barrier system to prevent air currents through the rest of the wall, blocks what water does get through the cladding from entering the structure, and provides means for rapid drying of the wall after the rain has stopped.

**Receptacle** An electrical wall outlet.

**Ridge vent** A roof ventilator that covers the entire ridge of the house, allowing air to escape from every one of the roof joist sections.

**Rigid foam insulation** Plastic insulating material that comes in rigid panels of various thicknesses and different properties. *See* Extruded polystyrene insulation.

**Sealer** A natural or chemical liquid applied to wood for waterproofing.

**Shellac** A wood finish derived from the lac beetle used to hide stains before painting.

**Shim** A small wedge-shaped piece of wood used to level or plumb a door or floor.

**Shingle** A thin small sheet of asphalt or wood overlapped on roofing and siding to provide protection from water.

**Siding** Protection for an exterior house wall made of aluminum, vinyl, wood, or stucco.

**Sill** A shelf installed at the bottom of a window.

**Soffit** The area under the eaves between the edge of the roof and the wall.

**Soffit vent** A vent that allows airflow into the attic from under the soffit.

**Solder** A low-melting-point alloy used to connect metal piping.

**Stud** A vertical wooden framing member.

**Subfloor** A base, typically plywood, installed under flooring material.

**Sump pump** A water pump designed to remove water from under the floor of a basement.

**Support wall** An interior wall that supports weight from the ceiling above.

**Thermal bridging** The flow of heat outside and cold inside a house through uninsulated structural members of windows, doors, walls and ceilings.

**Tongue-and-groove flooring** Flooring assembled from pieces with a tongue on one edge that fits into a groove on the opposite edge.

**Trisodium phosphate (TSP)** A cleaning agent used to prepare walls for painting.

**Truss** A framing structure designed to support weight over a large area.

**Tung oil** A wood finish derived from the oil of the Chinese tung tree.

**Undercoat** A base layer of paint designed to mask imperfections in the surface.

**Underlayment** Material applied over a subfloor to make the final floor level.

**Vapor barrier** Plastic or aluminum sheeting designed to block the diffusion of water vapor. Sometimes referred to as a moisture barrier.

**Varnish** A mixture of oil and resin used as a wood finish.

**Vent** A duct that allows for the intake and exhaust of air within a house.

**Wainscot** A molding that rises part way up an interior wall.

**Washer** A metal or rubber ring that prevents friction in metal joints.

**Water table** The natural level of water saturation in the soil.

**Weather stripping** Materials applied to the edges of doors and windows to reduce air and water leakage.

**Weep hole** A small hole found at the bottom of exterior brick walls that allows water trapped behind the wall to escape.

# Index

# N

Nails, removing from concrete, 51

# O

Odors
  basement odors, 85
  sewer odors, 82
  sink odors, 85
  smoke from outside, 99
  varathane, 144
Oiling wood ceilings, 65
Outlets. *See* Receptacles

# P

Pad applicators, 165
Paint
  acrylic, 39, 136
  all-acrylic, 166
  anti-slip additive, 142
  and asthma, 136
  cementitious paint, 39, 184
  containing fungicides, 118
  decor paint, 177
  latex, 39, 136, 137, 185
  oil-based, 137
  peeling paint, 142
  removing, from concrete, 53
  stain block, 139, 140, 143
  super-adherent primers, 51, 137, 143
Painting, 135
  brick foundations, 39
  brushes, 177
  ceramic tiles, 143
  crumbling concrete, 39
  hardboard, 139
  knots, 140, **140**

latex over oil-based paint, 137
  over oiled wood, 138
  over stained walls, 139
  over wallpaper, 138
  with pad applicators, 165
  with paint gloves, 27, **27,** 146
  paneling, 51
  siding, 165, 166
  spindles, 146
  with spray guns, 145, **145,** 165
  stucco, 143
  tools, 26-27, 177
  trowels, 55
  wrought iron, 149
Paint strippers, 148, **148,** 149
Paneling, 51
Parging, 35, 186
Pipe cutters, 24, **24**
Pipe rollers, 27, **27**
Pipes. *See* Plumbing
Pipes, water heating system, 105
Plaster, 186
  cracks, 49, 50, **50**
  holes, 48, *48*
Pliers, 18, **18,** 19, **19**
Plumbing, 67, *68, 71, 76,* **80**
  bathtubs, 75
  drain pipes, 79, 81
  faucets, 70, **70**
  frozen pipes, 83
  hot water tanks, 74, **74**
  noisy pipes, 81
  odors, 82, 85
  pipe types, 69
  plungers, 71
  rusty pipes, 74
  showers, 75, 76, *76,* 77, **77,** 82, 83

sinks, 71, *71,* 78, 82, 85
  soldering pipes, 78, **78**
  stack pipes, 79
  sump pumps, 84, **84,** 187
  toilets, 72, **72,** 73, 81
  tools, 24-25
  vent pipes, 79, 82
  water pressure, 69, 76, *76*
Plywood, 58, 186
Power hoses, 164, **164**
Pressure-treated wood, 146, 147
Primers, super-adherent, 35, 51, 137, 143, 186
Primers, vapor barrier, 137, 186
Professionals, 175, *175*
Profile gauges, 14, **14**
Propane torches, 25, **25**

# R

Radiators, 109, **109**
"Rain screen wall" principle, 153, 155, *155,* 186
Receptacles, 186
  air drafts, 89, **89**
  GFCIs, 88, **88,** 185
  replacing, 88, **88**
Resilient bars, 32, 63
R-factor, 33
Ridge vents, 159, **159,** 186
Roofs, 151
  drip-edges, 163
  flat-top roofs, 154, 157
  ice dams, 157, 158, **158,** 185
  mold, 162
  shingles, 162, 163
  vents, 117, **117,** 159, **159,** 186

# Measurement

## Lumber Widths and Thicknesses

Lumber is ordered by thickness, width, and length. When you order in imperial measurements (2 inches x 4 inches x 8 feet, for example), the thickness and width figures (in this instance 2 x 4) refer to nominal size—the dimensions of the piece as it left the saw. But what you get is the smaller, actual size remaining when the piece has been planed smooth; in actual fact, a piece $1^1/_2$ inches x $3^1/_2$ inches x 8 feet. (Length is not reduced by the processing.)

Metric measurements always describe the actual dimensions of the processed piece.

| Imperial (in.) nominal size (actual size) | | Metric (mm) actual size |
|---|---|---|
| 2 x 2 | $(1^1/_2$ x $1^1/_2)$ | 38 x 38 |
| 2 x 4 | $(1^1/_2$ x $3^1/_2)$ | 38 x 89 |
| 2 x 6 | $(1^1/_2$ x $5^1/_2)$ | 38 x 140 |
| 2 x 8 | $(1^1/_2$ x $7^1/_4)$ | 38 x 184 |
| 2 x 10 | $(1^1/_2$ x $9^1/_4)$ | 38 x 235 |
| 4 x 4 | $(3^1/_2$ x $3^1/_2)$ | 89 x 89 |
| 4 x 6 | $(3^1/_2$ x $5^1/_2)$ | 89 x 140 |

## Metric Plywood Panels

Plywood panels come in two standard metric sizes: 1200 millimetres x 2400 millimetres and 1220 millimetres x 2400 millimetres (the equivalent of a 4 foot x 8 foot panel). Other sizes are available on special order. With sheathing and select sheathing grades, metric and imperial thicknesses are generally identical. The metric sanded grades, however, come in a new range of thicknesses.

Metric thicknesses

| Sheathing and Select Grades | | Sanded Grades | |
|---|---|---|---|
| 7.5 mm | $(^5/_{16}$ in.) | 6 mm | $(^4/_{16}$ in.) |
| 9.5 mm | $(^3/_8$ in.) | 8 mm | $(^5/_{16}$ in.) |
| 12.5 mm | $(^1/_2$ in.) | 11 mm | $(^7/_{16}$ in.) |
| 15.5 mm | $(^5/_8$ in.) | 14 mm | $(^9/_{16}$ in.) |
| 18.5 mm | $(^3/_4$ in.) | 17 mm | $(^2/_3$ in.) |
| 20.5 mm | $(^3/_5$ in.) | 19 mm | $(^3/_4$ in.) |
| 22.5 mm | $(^7/_8$ in.) | 21 mm | $(^{13}/_{16}$ in.) |
| 25.5 mm | (1 in.) | 24 mm | $(^{15}/_{16}$ in.) |

## Carpeting

To estimate your carpeting needs in square metres:

1. Measure the room's longest and widest walls (include doorways and alcoves), adding 7.5 centimetres to each wall for good measure. Your calculation will be something such as: 5.18 metres + 7.5 centimetres = 5.26 metres (width); 5.79 metres + 7.5 centimetres = 5.87 metres (length)

2. Calculate the area of the room (5.26 metres x 5.87 metres = 30.87 square metres) You will need 31 m² to cover the room.

# Tiles and Tiling

This formula (based on 23-centimetre-square tiles and a room 5 metres long by 4 metres wide) will help you determine how many ceramic tiles you need to cover a room:

1. Divide 100 centimetres (1 metre) by 23 (100 ÷ 23 = 4.35 tiles per metre)
2. Find the number of tiles per side by multiplying length and width respectively by tiles per metre (5 x 4.35 = 21.75; 4 x 4.35 = 17.4)
3. Calculate the area *in tiles* (21.75 x 17.4 = 378.45, or about 380 tiles)
4. Add 10% for fitting (380 + 10% = 418)

# Paneling and Wallpapering

Calculating panel needs: On graph paper draw a scale model of the room you plan to sheet-panel. Let each square represent 30 cm². Measure the height of the walls; then sketch them on the plan, flopping them out from the floor so that they look like the dropped sides of a box.

Wall paneling sheets are usually 1200 mm x 2400 mm. Measure the room's perimeter (here 5.5 m x 2 + 6 m x 2 = 23 m or 23,000 mm) and divide by 1200 mm (the panel width). The result—19—is the number of panels needed for a room with a 2.4-metre-high ceiling.

How much wallpaper to buy: As with paneling:

1. Measure the room's perimeter: (length x 2) + (width x 2).
2. Multiply the perimeter by the height of the wall (to get the exact number of square metres).
3. It wallpapering the ceiling also, calculate the ceiling area (length x width = square metres).
4. Add areas of wall and ceiling to get the total area being wallpapered.
5. Count and measure all doors and windows.
6. Take all these measurements to your dealer to estimate the number of rolls needed for the job.

# Calculating Concrete Requirements

Multiply length by width to get the slab area in square metres. Then read across, under whichever of three thicknesses you prefer, to see how many cubic metres of concrete you will need.

| Area in square metres (m²) (length x width) | Thickness in millimetres | | |
| --- | --- | --- | --- |
| | 100 | 130 | 150 |
| | volume in cubic metres (m³) | | |
| 5 | 0.50 | 0.65 | 0.75 |
| 10 | 1.00 | 1.30 | 1.50 |
| 20 | 2.00 | 2.60 | 3.00 |
| 30 | 3.00 | 3.90 | 4.50 |
| 40 | 4.00 | 5.20 | 6.00 |
| 50 | 5.00 | 6.50 | 7.50 |

If a greater volume of concrete is required, multiply by the appropriate number. To lay a 100-millimetre-thick patio in an area 6 metres wide and 10 metres long, for example, estimate as follows: 6 metres x 10 metres = 60 metres square = area. Using the chart above, simply double the concrete quantity for a 30-metre-square, 100-millimetre-thick slab (2 x 3 m³ = 6 m³) or add the quantities for 10 m² and 50 m² (1 m³ + 5 m³ = 6 m³).

# Sources

**Aeroflo Inc.**
1-800-779-4021
world wide web: http://www.aeroflo.com
*In-line fans*

**Canada Mortgage and Housing Corporation (CMHC)**
world wide web: http://www.cmhc-schl.gc.ca
1-800-668-2642
*Pamphlets and publications on making homes healthier*

**Canadian Gypsum Company**
world wide web: http://www.cgcinc.com
*Sheet goods*

**Canadian Home Builders Association**
world wide web: http://www.chba.ca
*Information on building codes and working with construction professionals*

**Canadian Wood Council**
1-800-463-5091
world wide web: http://www.cwc.ca
*Publications on the design and use of wood products in construction*

**Dow Chemical Company**
1-800-395-1143
world wide web: http://www.dow.com
*Videos, pamphlets and publications on working with sheet insulation*

**The Institute for Research in Construction**
National Research Council of Canada
(613) 993-2607
world wide web: http://www.nrc.ca/irc
*Information on improving the quality, safety, and durability of Canadian homes*

**Moen Inc. Canada**
1-800-465-6130
world wide web: http://www.moen.com
*Faucets and pressure-balancing shower systems*

**Natural Resources Canada**
1-800-387-2000
world wide web: http://www.eeb-dee.nrcan.gc.ca
*Pamphlets and publications on heating, ventilation, and insulation*

**Union Energy**
1-800-774-2222
e-mail: email@unionenergy.ca
*Water- and air-treatment products*

# Acknowledgments

The editors would like to thank the following people for their contributions to **Just Ask Jon Eakes:**

**Reader's Digest**
Yves Lachance
Jacques Perrault

**Les Productions Interface**
Yang-Hai Eakes
François Beausoleil
Tommy Fortin
Marie-Ève Dumais

**VCR Active Media**
Bill Thompson
Bruno Palozzi
Tim Chan

**Photo Credits**
Cover: Stephen Homer

**Film work by**
Stanmont Inc.

**CD-ROM mastered and duplicated by**
VCR Active Media

**Printed & bound by**
Friesens

# How to Use the CD-ROM

## PC

We recommend running Just Ask Jon Eakes on a PC with Windows 95 and a 75 MHz Pentium processor or better. You will also need a 16-bit color display, a 16-bit sound card, 8 MB of available RAM, and a 6x speed CD-ROM drive.

• The CD-ROM is set to auto-run under Windows 95. If you want to manually start the program, click on the file RDIGEST.EXE found in the root directory of the disk.

• For optimum performance, it is recommended you quit all other open applications before you start the CD-ROM.

• To ensure the Internet hotlinks work smoothly, make sure you are connected to the Internet before starting the CD, and that you have allocated enough memory to your web browser.

• If you experience problems running the animations, you may have an older version of QuickTime for Windows installed on your machine. If this is the case, run the program QT32INST.EXE to have the disk automatically install QuickTime version 2.1.2 on your PC.

## Mac

We recommend running Just Ask Jon Eakes on a Mac with System 7.0 or greater and a PowerPC processor. You will also need a color display, 8 MB of available RAM, and a 6x speed CD-ROM drive.

• If you are using a Power Mac, click on the file Just Ask (PPC). For older Macs, click on Just Ask (68K).

• For optimum performance, quit all other open applications before you start the CD-ROM. If you find startup slow, disable all extensions apart from QuickTime.

• To ensure the Internet hotlinks work smoothly, make sure you are connected to the Internet before starting the CD, and that you have allocated enough memory to your web browser.

• If you experience problems running the animations, you may have an older version of QuickTime installed on your machine. If this is the case, update to QuickTime version 2.5 by running the file QTMac from the CD-ROM.